"I had the pleasure and privilege of working with Al DelBello when I served as commissioner of planning and economic development for the city of Yonkers. He was an amazing person. His intelligence, wit, and sense of humor as we worked through his clients' complex real estate issues were unrivaled. It was a joy to work with him, and I grew to love him in the process. I am not sure many politicians or former politicians elicit similar feelings."

Wilson Kimball – *President and CFO of the Municipal Housing Authority of the City of Yonkers*

D1225577

"Al DelBello was a visionary who worked tirelessly in his public and private sector life to make these visions a reality for the city of Yonkers, county of Westchester and the state of New York."

Ed Sheeran – *Palmer Economic Development Inc. and President and former Executive Director of YIDA*

"Al was the rare public official who worked to efficiently and creatively run county government while simultaneously anticipating future needs. He set the standard for effective and ethical county executive conduct. He was able to bring significant permanent solutions to Westchester with a bi-partisan approach that is desperately missing today in our national government."

Dick Ottinger – *Former Westchester Congressman and Dean of the Elisabeth Haub School of Law at Pace University*

"Both in 1976 as Westchester County Executive and in 1997 as chair of the Westchester County Health Care Corporation, Alfred DelBello played key roles in the birth and preservation of Westchester Medical Center: the primary teaching hospital of New York Medical College. This preserved the ability of our 162-year-old college to generate and disseminate knowledge about the causes, prevention and treatment of human disease and disabilities."

Edward C. Halperin, M.D. MA - *Chancellor/CEO and Professor of Radiation Oncology, Pediatrics and History at the New York Medical College of Touro University*

"Al had a strong belief about the difference in serving in executive office versus legislative office. When I urged him to run for the U.S. Senate, he said, 'No, I prefer hands-on – getting things done.'"

Ed Meyer - *Retired New York State Assemblyman and Connecticut State Senator*

ALFRED B. DELBELLO

HIS LIFE AND TIMES

He made the right things happen

BY JOHN A. LIPMAN

atmosphere press

Published by Atmosphere Press

Cover design by Ronaldo Alves

atmospherepress.com

DEDICATION

No one could have predicted that this book about Alfred B. DelBello would take on so much more meaning because of the lack of bipartisanship in our national government and politics in general, which commenced early in this 21st century. Forty years ago, a young man driven not by ambition, but rather a passion for doing the right things with a creative, professional government comprising men and women regardless of their political persuasion. He was persuaded by accomplishments and tackling challenges others in public office might shy away from, fearing loss of votes and favor from their constituents.

I dedicate this book to all those government officials and staff who believed in Al DelBello and stood by him, and helped with the outstanding achievements of his tenure. Some were ground-breaking, some brought national attention, but all brought stature and immense credibility to Westchester County.

Among the many allies in the DelBello government, one person stands out for her competence, dedication and, most important – her genuine friendship. Peggy Lichtenstein has been tenacious, supportive and relentless in her inspiration.

With an uncanny memory of the outstanding moments in government, which she was part of, she guided the research and moved the project along for seven years. Thank you, Peggy.

Thanks to editor Georgette Gouveia, an author herself, whose writing ability brought confidence to those of us who were patiently awaiting the completion of this book. Thank you, Georgette.

Thanks to author John Lipman for his diligence and persistent pursuit of the facts and pertinent details. Among those who attempted to write Al's biography, John was the only one who succeeded in portraying the creative government official, family man, and my husband. Thank you, John.

– Dee DelBello

EDITOR'S NOTE

Climate change. Health care. Race relations. Affordable housing. Education. Infrastructure. Police and prison reform. Workers' and women's rights.

These are some of the searing issues of our day. But a half-century ago, they also defined the political career of Alfred B. DelBello (1934-2015), first as mayor of Yonkers, New York; then as Westchester County Executive and finally as New York State Governor Mario M. Cuomo's first lieutenant governor.

As mayor of his native Yonkers – the largest city in Westchester, the county immediately north of New York City – he defied an ingrained, corrupt, inefficient patronage system to bring fiscal sanity and better living conditions to all Yonkers' citizens. (In an age when politicians ranging from former New York state Gov. Andrew Cuomo to British Prime Minister Boris Johnson have come under fire for allegedly mixing the public and the personal, DelBello was scrupulous in keeping both separate.)

As the first member of the Democratic Party to be elected Westchester County Executive, he created the first Office for the Disabled and the first Office for Women in New York State.

DelBello again balanced fiscal conservatism with quality-of-life issues – helping to open Westchester Medical Center in Valhalla and a waste recovery plant in Peekskill; building the county's only boat-launching ramp on Long Island Sound at Glen Island Park in New Rochelle; and creating bicycle paths along the Bronx River Parkway. His love of the environment and concern for health care in particular make him a not-so-"distant mirror," to borrow a term from historian Barbara Tuchman of our own times.

This, then, is no "He was born in a log cabin" biography but rather a look at the political and professional life of a man who, despite a public career, remained private.

I went to lunch with Al several times toward the end of his life when I went to work for Westfair Communications Inc., owned by his wife, Dee DelBello. It was in 2011 that the idea for this book first emerged, and I, as a potential author, talked about it with him over several lunches at the Renaissance Westchester Hotel in Harrison. Sadly, although we had collected and cataloged Al's experiences and memories of his life, the book would become a posthumous project when Al died of complications from a fall on May 15, 2015, after a brief, intense illness.

The Al I got to know at those lunches and at Westfair's office – where he would stop in and chat with the staff, enjoying a few of the candies they kept out front and playing with the West Highland Terriers that accompanied Dee to work – was a real mensch, a gentleman and gentle man who spoke warmly of his family, including son Damon, a pediatric orthopedic surgeon at Westchester Medical Center in Valhalla; daughter-in-law Jill; and grandchildren, Daniel, Alexandra, and Gabriella. But that warmth was especially reserved for Dee, whose smart sophistication was a source of great pride for him.

"Perhaps the greatest advice he shared with me, and

something I've always adhered to is, always make sure you get home and spend quality time with your family," former Westchester County Executive and New York State Republican gubernatorial hopeful Rob Astorino said when Al died. "The job is hectic, but always make time for your family."

Al understood that as important as politics was, it wasn't everything. And yet he believed the political arena was the only one in which you could affect wholesale change.

"I always enjoyed government," he said. "I was in it a long time and always felt it was the only place you could make a difference in people's lives. When I was in the business world, I would read about public issues, and I felt something was missing because I couldn't (affect) it."

Those remarks came in 1994 when he made an unsuccessful attempt at a comeback, running for a State Senate seat in Westchester County against a Republican tide and an opponent who would later be convicted of fraud. By then, he had been out of politics for almost ten years, resigning as lieutenant governor on Feb. 1, 1985.

Why did a man who thought the world of a field in which his star was ascending walk away from it? Readers will see that this had as much to do with the political system as it did with his fraught relationship with Mario Cuomo.

The irony: A man who, as a centrist Democrat, prided himself on working across party lines would see his political career done in by party politics.

More irony: DelBello then turned to the private sector, where he was able to have an effect on many of the issues he held dear, particularly the environment.

Ultimately, this is the story of a man who went on to pursue many of his political passions in business and, in so doing, become what Socrates would've called "a citizen of the world."

– **Georgette Gouveia**

CHAPTER ONE

Flyover Country

December 1984 – The Japanese businessmen were not pleased. Standing in a secure building in a terminal at La Guardia International Airport in Queens, they waited – ten minutes, twenty minutes, a half-hour as bursts of bitter cold swirled across the runways under a thick pall of indifferent gray, portending the kind of early-winter storm that periodically battered New York's urban archipelago with heavy snow. The undulating gusts churned the brine of Flushing Bay, infusing the sweet, heady kerosene vapors from idling jet engines with a dank, icy musk.

The men were part of the Keidanren, a postwar organization representing scores of Japanese companies, industrial organizations and regional economic groups. In the early 1980s, the Keidanren was riding the wave of Japanese economic dominance, crystallized in the number of Japanese imports that flooded the American markets at a time when the United States was still feeling the effects of a recession characterized by gas shortages, fourteen percent-plus interest rates and almost eleven percent unemployment. The proliferation of modern, electric-fired steel mills in east Asia had cratered coal-dependent Midwestern smelters, hobbling America's antiquated automobile industry in particular. Amid the economic downturn and runaway inflation of the 1970s, New York State had suffered greatly.

Accompanying the businessmen was a man determined to reverse the Japanese import tide and help restore American manufacturing pride. Alfred B. "Al" DelBello was, at 40, the lieutenant governor of New York, the so-called "Empire State." Lieutenant governors, like American vice presidents or spares to royal heirs, play a somewhat ceremonial role. Perhaps John Nance Garner, who served as President Franklin Delano Roosevelt's vice president from 1933 to 1941, spoke for "vices" and lieutenants everywhere when he said his job wasn't "worth a bucket of warm piss." For the accomplishment-oriented DelBello, being number two to Governor Mario M. Cuomo – a charismatic figure who was expected to ride his oratorical skills all the way to the White House or at least the United States Supreme Court – was equally challenging.

Still, DelBello reveled in his role as president of the State Senate, working across party lines just as he had done as mayor of Yonkers and Westchester County executive. He made the most of his ribbon-cutting duties and other opportunities. For almost a year, he had wooed businessmen in Asia, and the Keidanren in particular, seeking to drive Japanese car and train plants to New York State. In this, DelBello was helped by his elegant wife, Dee, whom Geoff Thompson of the public relations firm Thompson & Bender in Briarcliff Manor, New York, once described, along with her husband, as the "Jack and Jackie (Kennedy) of the county." As regional public relations director of Bloomingdale's in White Plains, the seat of Westchester government, and host of a WFAS-FM radio show from the store's Place Elegante department, Dee Del-Bello had engineered many foreign country events at Bloomingdale's White Plains and Stamford, Connecticut, locations.

Now members of the Keidanren – who had spent the morning touring New York City and the Port Authority of New York and New Jersey's facilities – were primed to meet with the governor himself, as he was scheduled to pick them up at La Guardia on his way from a Washington, D.C. meeting to Albany, the state capital. After the plane meeting, DelBello would lead the businessmen on a tour of the state legislature before a banquet at Rensselaer Polytechnic Institute's museum.

The problem was that no governor appeared on the runway apron. Amid the pitched whistling of turbine engines, DelBello's carefully anchored calm masked a growing apprehension. He called Michael J. Del Giudice, Cuomo's chief of staff and later adviser to Cuomo's son Andrew during his tenure as New York governor, only to learn that the governor had decided to fly directly to Albany, then have the plane turn around to pick them up.

The Japanese are famed for their punctuality and politesse. But the delegation grew visibly upset at what it saw as a breach of etiquette.

What to do? Moving quickly to try and salvage the day, DelBello reassured the businessmen, pressing on with the state legislature tour and Rensselaer banquet – to no avail. As he swirled the last of the Cabernet Sauvignon in his glass during the evening meal, DelBello could only feign interest in a conversation that he knew would go nowhere. There would be no multibillion-dollar Japanese investment in New York. For DelBello, it would be the last salvo in his disappointing relationship with the governor, born of a "shotgun marriage" on his long, fateful road to Albany.

CHAPTER TWO

When Mario 'Met' Al

Long before there was Kathy Hochul – the lieutenant governor who succeeded Andrew Cuomo as the first female governor of New York State on August 24, 2021, after he resigned amid allegations that he sexually harassed women – there was Mary Ann Krupsak. Krupsak served as lieutenant governor to Hugh Carey, who was first elected governor in 1974.

New York is one of eighteen states where party nominations for governor and lieutenant governor are made independently of each other. Candidates for each position run in their own primary campaigns. The winners run together on the final party ticket. Usually, a popular governor running for re-election would throw his or her support to the existing lieutenant. The party would then dutifully rally around that ticket at the June convention. Yet the voters had the final say in the September primary.

Whether the result of philosophical differences or political opportunism – reportedly, Krupsak was upset at the way

Carey treated her and disliked the political anonymity typical of the lieutenant governor's position – she decided to challenge Carey for the governorship in 1978. On such decisions do careers turn, for her power play would have a profound effect on Mario Cuomo's and DelBello's professional paths and thorny relationship.

Ironically, Krupsak had defeated then-political novice Cuomo for the lieutenant governorship in 1974. (As a consolation and perhaps to keep Cuomo out of the next gubernatorial contest, Carey brought him aboard his administration as secretary of state.) Ultimately, however, Krupsak would accuse Carey of "lacking integrity and ability." It seemed an odd thing to say about a man who had helped liberate a German concentration camp in World War II before becoming the devoted father of fourteen children. The seven-term congressman ran for governor in 1974, having just lost his beloved first wife, Helen, to cancer. He pushed on, driving from town to town throughout the state with his family in a Winnebago. As governor, he would bail New York City out of a financial collapse, a pivotal decision that turned the Big Apple around and started the famous "I Love New York" campaign. He was likable, decent and level-headed – personal qualities that would remind DelBello of James F.X. O'Rourke, his onetime opponent in the Yonkers mayoral race.

Carey favors DelBello

Needing to replace Krupsak in his bid for a second gubernatorial term in 1978, Carey favored DelBello. He had done remarkably well in his career, first as the gutsy, reforming mayor of Yonkers and then as the urbane Westchester County executive, teaming with the mayors of New York's other major cities to get the upper hand in state financial aid. He was a rising star. Carey not only admired him; he liked him.

Happy times with Governor Carey.

At the time of Krupsak's resignation, however, DelBello and his wife Dee were on vacation in Europe. He had been re-elected as county executive in 1977, as only state races took place in even-numbered years. They had decided to blow off the Democratic primary, figuring nothing newsworthy would happen. The couple had just landed in Amsterdam when Del-Bello got a call: Would he be available to run as Carey's lieutenant governor? DelBello said he would be glad to do so and would return to New York the next day if Carey asked.

Word spread that Carey was considering DelBello as his

running mate. But he was also considering Cuomo. The appointed secretary of state was a lawyer fluent in Greek and Italian but had never been elected to public office. Still, he had powerful party connections and a populist image as a blue-collar hero. That would be useful to Carey, especially upstate, after the potentially damaging departure of native daughter Krupsak.

Cuomo knew he had a chance to claim the lieutenant governor's position, but he would have to squeeze DelBello out of the picture. If Carey won the primary against Krupsak, which was likely, Cuomo might end up riding shotgun in the governor's limo. A networking master, Cuomo put on a full-court press with Democratic Party operatives. DelBello was still in Europe, making his own emergency politicking impossible.

A fateful pairing

Like many political decisions, this one would be brokered by a handful of the Democratic Party's most influential New Yorkers, including Brooklyn party leader Amadeo "Meade" Esposito, Carey attorney Judah Gribetz, political consultant David Garth and Ed Koch, the man who had beaten Cuomo in a bitter New York City mayor's race the previous year. Everyone gathered was in favor of DelBello as the lieutenant candidate, except for Garth. Understanding the Queens-born and reared Cuomo's appeal for New York City – the state and country's most populous city and a place where Carey's strength was middling – Garth prevailed upon Carey. Within a day, Cuomo had been chosen.

DelBello was disappointed but let it go, knowing he had a key role to play as Westchester's leader. He led a political bulwark in a majority-Republican county that would bolster Carey with bipartisan support. And several defining issues were still uncertain at that time, including the Westchester Medical Center and the waste-to-energy plant. Had they offered DelBello the lieutenant governor's slot, those critical projects may not have succeeded. Remaining in White Plains would give him a full second term to cultivate his influence and complete his legacy. Perhaps there would be another opportunity in four years.

Krupsak was quickly dispatched in the primary. The Carey-Cuomo ticket went on to win the governor's mansion in 1978. DelBello went on to complete a highly accomplished second term as county executive. Yet the secret was out: DelBello had been Carey's first choice for lieutenant governor. It was not something Cuomo was likely to forget.

In the fall of 1981, Carey was gearing up for his third run. Not wanting to risk another in-house rebellion, he had let Cuomo hold on to his influential position as secretary of state when taking the lieutenant governor's seat, enabling him to expand his scope of power and establish offices throughout the state. In short order, Cuomo built his budget to $1 million per year, close to double the amount under Krupsak's tenure.

But Carey was also weary of Cuomo's power-building. He had misgivings about not choosing DelBello as Krupsak's replacement three years earlier. Had Cuomo remained secretary of state, he would surely have balked at DelBello's appointment, but it would have been over quickly. With another election on the horizon, however, and Cuomo now looking over Carey's shoulder, any support for an alternative candidate would have to be done with great finesse.

Going up against a popular party influencer like Cuomo would be a challenge. But DelBello came with proven credentials that might make even Cuomo's blue-collar home district in Queens go for him. Certainly, DelBello's achievements in protecting Westchester's carpenters' union from financial collapse and keeping employment in Westchester three points above the national average had made him a standout. He had a thirteen-year record of achievement in elected executive positions. He was a people-person, a true, trusted leader. He was the guy voters would want in the lieutenant governor's office when Carey decided his time was done.

Late in 1981, DelBello made a phone call to Carey, catching up on several issues. DelBello's chief of staff happened to be in his office talking with him when the secretary informed DelBello that the governor was on the phone. DelBello spoke with Carey for several minutes, then interjected that he was considering a run for lieutenant governor. Carey seemed pleased.

"He wanted to let Carey know," DelBello's aide said. "Carey was certainly interested in him back in '78. It was clear the two of them liked each other. But word must have gotten back to Cuomo pretty fast that Al was pitching himself for the lieutenant governor's seat."

While DelBello loved Westchester, he worried he would grow dissatisfied – and perhaps politically irrelevant – if he didn't reach for the next rung on the ladder. He had always felt the governor's office was where he belonged. The primary would shake things out, he thought. Even if he lost, he would be seen as a future contender for the state's top slot. There would be other chances to climb.

In making this decision, DelBello had reflected on the beginning of his political career when he was a councilman in Yonkers. Tired of the corruption and domination by a Republican council, he thought his efforts to change government were hopeless. Yet he remembered his wife, Dee, encouraging him to run for mayor by saying, "What have you got to lose?"

DelBello's move would be thrown into sharp relief in January 1982 by some jaw-dropping news: Carey announced he would not seek re-election. His poll numbers were abysmal, no doubt in part because of his hasty, disastrous second marriage to real estate mogul Evangeline Gouletas, who had obfuscated details about her previous marital history, jeopardizing his standing with Roman Catholic voters, among others. Carey had already been challenged by a lieutenant governor and saw the possibility of it happening again. The word in Albany was that Cuomo wanted the top job and had threatened his own boss with a primary challenge.

Now fatigued by two terms and a long recession, as well as a lieutenant governor on the hunt, Carey called it quits. Immediately after he made his announcement, Cuomo was direct. "I said earlier that if he didn't run, I intended to run. Nothing has changed."

He added he was sticking to a rigid timetable of formally announcing his candidacy by mid-March. He made a much-delayed formal announcement in May – a pattern of Hamlet-like rumination and procrastination he would repeat in subsequent years.

Enter Ed Koch

Ed Koch exhibited no such indecision. The popular mayor of New York City announced his gubernatorial intentions in late February. Koch was a gregarious, garrulous contrast to Cuomo's somber, scholarly mien. He was irreverent and ebullient, a quintessential New Yorker. And he was the man who had defeated Cuomo in a bruising race to be New York's mayor five years earlier. But he had a weakness that grew more pronounced the farther he traveled from Manhattan.

Newspaper columnists described Koch as everything from being a candidate of "formidable assets" to one who spouted "loudmouth, smart-alecky folderol." He was indeed controversial and opinionated. Those were exactly the defiant traits that a financially battered New York City needed in the late 1970s. But they made him vulnerable upstate as a candidate for governor.

When Cuomo finally entered the race, he telephoned Del-Bello and told him he didn't want him on the ticket. It was a brash thing to say that revealed to DelBello that Cuomo fully expected him to win the primary contest for lieutenant governor. Cuomo downplayed the tension between them, telling him that if they both won their respective nominations, New Yorkers would never elect two downstate Italian American lawyers.

That may have had a ring of truth. Italian American politicians were still fighting an uphill battle in those days, contending with rumors of mob ties. But it was also clear that Cuomo remembered DelBello had been Carey's favorite son. Now Carey was gone, and Cuomo wanted DelBello out of the picture as well.

DelBello had no intention of backing down. He was running against Carl McCall, a man whom he had known and respected for many years. McCall was a popular black politician with a heavy pull in Manhattan's Harlem neighborhood but whose roots were in New England. He was born and raised in Boston's minority Roxbury neighborhood. He graduated from Dartmouth College, taught high school and served in the U.S. Army. Later, McCall attended Newton Theological School before moving to New York City to perform church outreach services. It was there he became involved in politics, ultimately serving three terms as state senator from Harlem before seeking the party's nomination for lieutenant governor.

DelBello and McCall had moments of conflict during the primary debates, as would be expected. DelBello had always vigorously advocated for the rights of black residents. He remembered his shock when serving in the National Guard at the boiling racism practiced in the south. He had some momentary hesitation about running against a black man in the primary, but he felt that the greatest expression of his belief in equality meant treating his political opponent like any other.

McCall, who would become state comptroller in 1993, was an experienced and smart state legislator. He was a good debater and pulled no punches. Neither did DelBello. The two men, fairly close in political philosophy, engaged one another in spirited exchanges. The voters would ultimately decide.

Throughout the campaign, DelBello had stated publicly that he would be happy to run with either gubernatorial candidate. He wanted to appear relatively neutral. But the press knew he was Koch's favorite. Cuomo had already thrown his support for McCall. The pairing of the candidates – along with the rivalries and divides – seemed inevitable.

With Hasidic rabbis in Borough Park, Brooklyn, during DelBello's campaign for lieutenant governor.

The convention took place in Syracuse. Koch was a rock star. His upstairs convention suite was mobbed with people. Well-wishers thronged the hallway, awaiting entry. Just fifty feet away, Cuomo opened the doors to his suite and stepped out. He looked at the crowd and announced with feigned sadness, "Doesn't anyone want to come visit me?" A few people in the Koch line laughed. One of Koch's waiting supporters smiled and said, "Well, Mr. Cuomo, do you have a bar in there?"

Cuomo tilted his head back in a boisterous laugh and said with a wide grin, "Sure, c'mon in." He shook the man's hand and began ushering voters through the door. Soon, both suites were filled. Intraparty politics were tossed aside as delegates and campaign supporters toasted both candidates, feeling for one brief, beautiful moment that the Democrats were united in purpose and destined for victory, regardless of who won the primary.

On June 22, 1982, the party convention gave Koch and DelBello the nod. It wasn't a surprise. But the race was far from over. A month before Koch announced his run, Playboy magazine interviewed him and published an earful of his urban bias. His acerbic comments about life outside New York City came across as arrogant and parochial. He called the suburbs "a sterile environment."

It was a big mistake, especially after three decades of urban out-migration that had turned the suburbs into a powerful voting bloc. To make matters worse, he referred to Albany, a city of a half-million people, as "small-town life at its worst." He dumped on rural upstate New York, calling it "a joke." It was, to say the least, bad political theater. Upstate Democrats were fuming and worried: They could only imagine what a Republican opponent would do with that in the general election.

The world would never know. In a stunning upset, primary voters rebelled against the Syracuse convention and elected Cuomo as the party's nominee in September, less than a week after many polls predicted an eleven-point victory for Koch. In a far less surprising outcome, DelBello received the lieutenant governor's nomination, landing the two men on the same ticket. Strong and popular among their own political demographics, the candidates won the general election against a bright, wealthy self-made businessman, Lewis Lehrman, president of Rite Aid pharmacies. It was daunting. Lehrman outspent them by almost three to one, making New York's gubernatorial race the most expensive in U.S. history at that time. But on November 2, 1982, the Cuomo-DelBello ticket eked out a 165,000-vote margin out of 5.25 million votes cast statewide.

A shotgun marriage

There was much to be cautiously optimistic about. Cuomo's no-holds-barred approach promised a hands-on executive who would carve his name in the Tuckahoe marble of Albany's State House, while DelBello's professional management style, steeped in cross-party cooperation, would forge inroads into the powerful Republican leadership controlling the state legislature. It was a match made in downstate New York, if not in heaven. It would work.

But trouble was brewing. On election night, after it was clear that the two men had taken the state's executive office, a jubilant, weary DelBello meandered down the hall of Manhattan's Sheraton Centre Hotel with his wife Dee and several others in tow to congratulate the governor-elect. Dee recalls the disquieting events.

"I remember election night when Al won the lieutenant

governor race, and Cuomo was elected governor. We went to the governor's hotel suite to congratulate him. Matilde (Cuomo's wife) opened the door after our knock and tried to be polite. We could see beyond her down a long hallway that Cuomo sat glued to a television screen. He didn't look up, didn't move. It was eerily uncomfortable, and I said to Al and his aides, 'Let's get out of here.'" After briefly mingling and sharing congratulations with others in the suite, he and his wife left, fearing an unworkable situation.

Though there had been tensions between them, DelBello was dismayed by the governor-elect's personal slight. He comforted himself by speculating that it had been a long night. He thought Cuomo would be more affable the next day. Perhaps he was lost in thought, distracted by all the activity in his suite and his focus on his acceptance speech. But it was, nevertheless, awkward and embarrassing.

Marching down New York's 5th Avenue during the Columbus Day Parade are (from left) Congressman Mario Biaggi, Mayor Ed Koch, Lieutenant Governor Mario Cuomo and County Executive Alfred DelBello in New York City on Oct. 11, 1982. (AP Photo)

A month earlier, DelBello had walked side-by-side with both Cuomo and Koch at the Columbus Day parade on New York's Fifth Avenue in a show of post-primary unity. He wasn't naïve enough to expect friendship from his political rival, but he had hoped for a manageable partnership.

Insiders had referred to the race as the Democrats' "shotgun wedding." Though they had never merged their offices prior to the general election, both men had been in it to win. Cuomo knew that DelBello's legendary managerial competence and enormous bipartisan appeal as the executive of one of New York's most populous, powerful counties – one that bordered New York City – was valuable to him.

Al and Dee both sat down the next morning with Ed Koch and David Garth, DelBello's friend and political strategist who himself had pushed Carey to choose Cuomo as his lieutenant governor in 1978. Dee asked: "Can Al refuse to be sworn in as lieutenant governor and stay on as county executive?" He still had one year left in his term. After hearing about Cuomo's mistreatment of DelBello on election night, Garth urged him to resign immediately as the lieutenant governor-elect. He could indeed stay on as county executive. Other opportunities would arise. It was a safe bet.

But DelBello would have none of it. He had made a pledge to the people of New York. Backing out now would be a betrayal. His service as lieutenant governor was about more than his political career. It was about making government work for the people he served. It always had been.

Things seemed sunnier a day or two later. An ecstatic Cuomo proclaimed that DelBello "will be the greatest lieutenant governor in the history of the state of New York." Several days after that, The New York Times trumpeted that "Westchester may have made the difference. Aided by running mate Alfred B. DelBello, the county executive, Mr. Cuomo won the normally G.O.P. county by 1,300 votes." That was an important revelation and one DelBello would think about for years to come. What if he had decided not to throw his hat into the ring this time around? Would Cuomo have won after all?

Despite the upbeat quotes in the papers, DelBello remained concerned about Cuomo's cold shoulder. He contacted Cuomo's son, Andrew – the man who would someday be governor himself – to set up a meeting with the governor-elect. A few days later, DelBello visited Cuomo in his transition headquarters at the World Trade Center in Manhattan. DelBello stepped into the office after being announced by Cuomo's secretary. Cuomo swiveled around in his chair and faced him in exasperated recognition, "You should be sitting in this seat," he said. DelBello was surprised. It was the first moment of honesty between the two men since the campaign began. DelBello felt sympathy for Cuomo. He tried to reassure him.

"Mario, if I had intended to be sitting in that seat, I would have run for governor," he said, trying to de-escalate a moment and a relationship that threatened to blow up. "My intention is to be as helpful and supportive as I can, and I will never say anything negative that would affect the governorship."

DelBello's choice of words was salient. He was politically loyal, but not to the person. He was loyal to the offices that he and Cuomo would hold and to the residents that those offices served. Cuomo understood that. His demeanor relaxed somewhat. He seemed momentarily comforted, less by what DelBello had said than by the realization that the inevitable confrontation was over. The two men spoke for several minutes about the inauguration and setting things up in Albany. The outward hostility had dissipated. But tension still hung in the air.

Afterward, DelBello had an idea. He had been impressed with Andrew Cuomo's work as campaign manager and transition coordinator. Andrew would not be joining his father in

Albany – a way to avoid the appearance of nepotism. DelBello asked Andrew if he would be his own chief of staff. He thought it would be a good way to ensure coordination between the governor's and lieutenant governor's offices. Andrew seemed interested and said he would talk to his father. Several days later, the answer came back. "Nope," Andrew said. "He didn't think that would be a workable solution." (Instead, Andrew would work for his father as a policy adviser for $1 a year.) Might the careers of all three men have been different had Andrew Cuomo taken the post?

The New Year's Day inauguration featured 4,000 people crowded into Albany's Empire State Plaza Convention Center, the first time in over five decades that the inauguration wasn't held in the Assembly chamber. Cuomo had chosen the location so he could invite a much larger crowd. Not surprisingly, he made a rousing speech with more than a dozen bursts of applause. As usual, there were thousands of handshakes and gestures of goodwill, buoyed by Aaron Copland's "Fanfare for the Common Man" and Neil Diamond's "America."

The new lieutenant governor in Albany taking the oath of office, with wife and son at his side.

But the celebratory fervor belied a simmering battle. When DelBello arrived at the New York State Capitol, he and his staff of ten were stopped at the door of the lieutenant governor's office in the executive suite, where Cuomo himself and many prior lieutenant governors had served. Told that the office "wasn't available," DelBello was directed to the lavish but small two-room suite that housed his other obligatory state function, the president of the State Senate. There was still no word on how many staffers DelBello could bring to Albany, but the people he already had with him were tripping over one another in the tiny office.

A surprising ally

He soon discovered that his budget was being cut from $1 million to $600,000. DelBello took it as nothing more than belt-tightening in difficult economic times, the kind of decision the fiscally conservative Democrat had made many times himself. Yet it would soon be cut to zero by the same man who, during the previous administration and a much worse fiscal crisis, had increased his own budget, expanded the scope of his powers and commanded a lavish staff of thirty-four people. DelBello's official functions and funding, including the politically powerful role of state ombudsman, were transferred to the secretary of state, Gail Shaffer. It was a squeeze-out.

State Senate Majority Leader Warren Anderson, a Republican, would have none of it. He had known DelBello for years as a man of great intelligence and fairness, even through their political disagreements. He immediately restored DelBello's salary and his staff support, though DelBello would remain in the Senate office. Once again, DelBello's reputation for bipartisan cooperation – something sorely missing in today's political divide – had cleared a space for him when his path had been blocked by his own party.

"You're one of us now," Anderson told the new president of the Senate. "We'll make sure you have what you need."

CHAPTER THREE

A Marriage of Inconvenience

With a click of a switch underneath the top of the lectern, DelBello turned on the lights in the State Senate chamber.

"Who says the lieutenant governor doesn't have power?" he said with a smile.

DelBello was preparing for his first day as president of the upper house of the legislature, the most visible part of his elected office. Having been given a downsized lieutenant governor's suite, DelBello knew this would be his true "home" in Albany.

He had had plenty of run-ins with the Republican-controlled Senate before, particularly during Senator Joseph R. Pisani's contentious campaign against him for the Westchester County Executive seat just fourteen months earlier. (After being indicted for tax evasion and fraud in 1983 and many up-and-down legal battles, Pisani would plead guilty to tax evasion in 1986 and be sentenced to one year in prison.)

Senate Majority Leader Warren Anderson had sided with

Pisani during his failed bid for Westchester county executive, an act of party loyalty DelBello had accepted as the political norm. Since he had been elected lieutenant governor, however, Anderson treated him as a colleague in Albany's political jungle, a place where only the governor, the senate majority leader, and the assembly majority leader held real power.

The ghosts of Attica

Exactly one week into DelBello's new role, the Cuomo Administration was staring down a riot at Sing Sing Correctional Facility in Ossining, in which prisoners in a cellblock revolted and took sixteen guards hostage. The section where the riot had started contained roughly 600 prisoners out of a total population of 2,150. The potential for a violent outcome was formidable.

Cuomo did not want a repeat of Attica, the specter of which still hung in the air. In the prison riot at the Attica Correctional Facility twelve years earlier, forty-three had died, including ten corrections hostages. A bloody end to the Sing Sing insurrection would mar the rest of Cuomo's governorship. He was lucky to have at his disposal a person who knew how to handle a prison uprising.

DelBello's experience in quelling the Westchester County Jail riot eighteen months earlier was still recent news. More than three hundred inmates had loosed themselves within the penitentiary building. Rather than rushing armed troops into the facility – as many Republicans, including Pisani, had demanded – DelBello had decided on a negotiated settlement. He and the county corrections commissioner went in themselves, without a police escort, and spoke with inmates about resolving overcrowding in the jail, among other needed reforms.

Within twenty-four hours, the situation was resolved. The inmates voluntarily returned to their cells without a single shot being fired.

Cuomo assembled a team in his Manhattan office, led by his son, Andrew. He never consulted DelBello and never included him in so much as a phone call, despite his offer to help. Dee remembers a tense call between Al and Cuomo late in the night when Cuomo told Al to back off and not interfere. During three tense days, Cuomo's team negotiated a truce, ending the uprising without bloodshed but not without irony: The first test of the new governor's mettle might have called for the involvement of an individual he seemed determined to ignore.

The risk manager

Cuomo set DelBello to work on other matters, including Westchester's now-defunct Indian Point Energy Center. On the banks of the Hudson River in Buchanan, the plant generated as much as fifteen percent of the electricity for the entire New York metropolitan region. It was opened in 1962 with additional power units added as late as the early 1970s.

But in recent years, a number of problems had arisen, including the buckling of the stainless-steel liner inside one of the new reactors, repeated releases of small amounts of radioactive water into the Hudson, and alarm-system failures. In one incident, engineers arrived at work to find nine feet of water inside one of the containment buildings, yet no alarm had been triggered. Several of these events occurred during the last few years of DelBello's county executive administration. Everyone, including DelBello, wanted the plant closed. The area around the power station was the most densely populated of any fallout zone in the United States.

As lieutenant governor, however, DelBello worked for an administration that wanted it kept open. Yet his desire for increasing public safety, regardless of Cuomo's stance on the plant, was paramount. Westchester was the leader in the related four-county nuclear preparedness zone mandated by the Federal Emergency Management Agency (FEMA). (The other counties included Putnam County to the north and Rockland and Orange counties on the west side of the Hudson.) As the former Westchester County Executive, DelBello coordinated FEMA's "no-notice" drills. If anything went wrong, he briefed the press. After several drills, FEMA considered the emergency evacuation program a success, giving high marks to the state team that DelBello managed.

Preventing youth suicide

Cuomo wanted the drills to work, but he didn't give DelBello much support. Yet DelBello was able to make progress on other issues that the governor would support. He addressed the teen suicide problem with great urgency, a matter with which he had grappled as county executive. Cuomo, himself a father of four, was indeed supportive. At DelBello's urging, Cuomo created New York's first council on youth suicide prevention. DelBello headed the council and later became chair of the national committee on youth suicide prevention.

The suicides of twelve young people in the northern suburbs of New York City helped attract national attention to the need for preventative measures. Westchester, Rockland and Putnam counties saw their rates climb dramatically. The national figures were equally striking. In the previous year, 6,000 people between the ages of fifteen and twenty-four had committed suicide. The council sought $3.5 million to be earmarked for statewide programs that would train educators, parents and students to be aware of the warning signs.

So passionate was DelBello about this issue that he wrote an opinion piece in The New York Times. He asked why the problem was growing so rapidly among youth and what parents, teachers and society in general could do about it. He argued that sweeping the problem under the rug or blaming it on single causes like drugs and alcohol only made it worse. His frankness was unequivocal:

"We must look the problem straight in the eye and respond on behalf of those thousands of young people who will otherwise choose death over life. The more rapidly we act, the more lives we will save."

DelBello also devoted himself to bolstering the state's economy, as he had done for Westchester County. He created a network of regional economic development councils throughout the state, which in turn created jobs suitable to each region's economic strengths and cultural assets. He promoted economic development among New York's Native American

Lieutenant Governor DelBello touring New York state for the rebuilding campaign.

nations. Because of rapid changes in New York's economy, he established a Plant Closing Task Force to make industrial closings more predictable. He also started a plant employee job training program, including job training for the homeless that would deal with drug and alcohol problems, mental health challenges and promote greater self-sufficiency.

Hometown hero

In urging New York's economic revitalization, he didn't forget his hometown. By 1984, Yonkers was once again in a fiscal crisis – and once again, his longtime rival, Angelo Martinelli, was mayor after a two-year hiatus. Yonkers was fortunate to have a native son in the lieutenant governor's office. The city was facing severe shortfalls that had not been previously reported to the public – a $9.5 million deficit in that fiscal year and up to a $40 million deficit in the following year.

DelBello spurred the governor to provide badly needed assistance, and the governor agreed. Cuomo created the State Panel on Yonkers City Finances, along with an Emergency Financial Control Board that would provide a large advance to the city to keep schools open. He appointed DelBello as chairman. The panel advocated for state enabling legislation to create independent school districts free from the city's financial chaos. Other state legislation created an income tax surcharge to manage the debt.

Yet DelBello remained increasingly frustrated by what he saw as himself being ostracized by the governor. It wasn't just the smaller quarters outside the state capitol building, the smaller budget, or the sputtering car they forced him to use that sometimes broke down on its way to important state events. Cuomo had stripped him of the state ombudsman role

– the powerful tool that allowed the lieutenant governor to do favors for state residents – and given it to Secretary of State Gail Shaffer. And he denied DelBello the opportunity to serve in a side role as chairman of the Metropolitan Transportation Authority (MTA). Through it all, DelBello took it on the chin, even as he was squeezed out of budgeting and commerce issues. But all men have their breaking point.

Japan calling

The final straw for DelBello would be Cuomo's flyover of the Japanese business delegation in early December 1984. One of DelBello's key initiatives was getting Asian companies to invest in New York. In April 1983, he planned a trade mission to Asia with stops in Taiwan, Hong Kong and Japan. He said that he had spoken with the governor, who had approved the trip. But Tim Russert, Cuomo's spokesman and future host of NBC's "Meet the Press," said that the governor had "no opinion" about the trip and that the lieutenant governor was free to travel as an independent official.

By July, DelBello had developed a relationship with Hino Motors in Japan to propose building buses in New York. DelBello said he was optimistic about the plan, which would have included the construction of a new Hino plant in the state.

"It sounds like one of the best opportunities New York State is ever going to have to start a whole new industry," DelBello said.

Previous deals with bus manufacturers for New York City had been stymied by federal design requirements, including access for the disabled. A disastrous $89 million deal with Grumman Corp. five years earlier had produced 851 "lemons"

Lieutenant Governor DelBello meeting with a member of the Keidanren in Japan.

that had to be retired because of constant cracks in the under-carriage. Hino buses were tested and performed admirably, but they had a problem: The seats weren't wide enough for ample American derrières. The demonstration models were eventually returned to the manufacturer, and another model was chosen.

While the trade mission was a success, the invitation for Asian investors to visit New York would prove DelBello's swan song. After almost a year of Asian business recruitment, he had successfully enticed the Keidanren – Japan's top business executives – to come to the United States. The group had billions to invest. They were impressed with his presentation and decided New York would be their first stop in December 1984. DelBello had arranged for Cuomo to fly to New York's

LaGuardia International Airport from Washington, D.C., where he was attending a meeting. The governor would host the delegation on the flight to Albany, then join them later for dinner at Rensselaer Polytechnic Institute's museum after the DelBello-led tour of the state legislature. But Cuomo never showed up. He flew over LaGuardia without stopping.

After DelBello made the urgent call to Michael J. Del Giudice, Cuomo's chief of staff, the plane returned empty, and DelBello tried to piece together the proverbial remains of the day.

As the executives prepared themselves for the dinner, DelBello stopped by Del Giudice's office. He was visibly upset.

"Mike," he said. "These executives are expecting to meet with the governor. You agreed to this." Del Giudice sighed, revealing some frustration with the governor's slight.

DelBello continued: "Look, the governor walks to the mansion right past the museum. Why don't you have him stop in and say hello to these people? They're investing billions of dollars in the United States, and they've come to New York State first." The two agreed Del Giudice would talk with Cuomo.

But Cuomo never stopped by, even just to shake their hands. He ghosted them – just like he had ghosted DelBello on election night. The executives continued their travel to other states, where they invested billions in automobile manufacturing and plastics. But because of the governor's slight, they never invested in New York. Not a single worker in the state, most of whom had voted for Cuomo, ever saw a dime from what could have been a gold mine for New York's economic woes.

But they never knew about it. DelBello had promised the governor that he would never say or do anything that would distract from helping the people of New York. Cuomo's no-show that night certainly upset Del Giudice and Senate

Majority Leader Warren Anderson. But no one was more upset than DelBello.

"My reaction to what the governor did to the Keidanren Association so discouraged me that I decided I had to resign as lieutenant governor," he said. "I just couldn't continue to exist under that falsity."

On December 7, DelBello announced his resignation, earning the jocular reference in the press as his "Pearl Harbor Day." It would take effect in February. It was only the second time in the state's history that a lieutenant governor had resigned. In 1953, Lieutenant Governor Frank C. Moore had left amid a political dispute with Governor Thomas E. Dewey after Dewey had swung his support for another candidate in the primary. DelBello wasn't going to wait around for that to happen.

"It's easy to get suckered into pretending you're important," he said at the time. "I wasn't about to pretend."

With presidential candidate Walter Mondale in Westchester.

DelBello figured it was the right call. Logic and his own steady, rational temperament might have dictated playing the long game – maybe give it a couple of years to see if Cuomo might run for president. But Cuomo might have tried to bump him off the 1986 primary ticket. In the interim, DelBello would have had to endure more exclusion.

Prior to the November 1984 presidential election, DelBello was asked what would happen if Democratic presidential candidate Walter Mondale lost. (Mondale would lose to Ronald Reagan 59% to 41%.) DelBello suggested that Cuomo would be a good candidate in 1988. When asked about the comment, Cuomo responded, "He's supporting himself so vigorously at the moment, I'm not sure he'll need any support from me. His most recent statements urging me on were at the very best unseemly, at the very worst impetuous."

It sounded like DelBello had made a gaffe, but he hadn't. His statement was calculated, but also true. He believed Cuomo would be a good presidential candidate and, if successful, the governorship would become his.

A fateful breakup

As always, the Cuomo-DelBello marriage of political inconvenience was a topsy-turvy affair. Several months earlier, during what was being hailed in the press as a budding political romance between the two men, Cuomo had appeared at a fundraising event for DelBello to express "the enormous respect and admiration and gratitude I have for the lieutenant governor." Yet, at the same time, Cuomo's top aides were intentionally putting out the word that DelBello "would make a marvelous candidate for state comptroller." In the middle of his second year in office, this was the equivalent of saying,

"Don't let the door hit you on your way out."

The writing had been on the wall during a mid-year interview when Cuomo had praised DelBello's ability and acknowledged that the post of lieutenant governor was "difficult and frustrating." But he added, "He obviously chose Koch over me. He had to adjust to his own disillusioned expectations. It's been a little difficult, but he's coming along now." It was a condescending pat on the head that felt more like a slap in the face. Cuomo simply could not let things go.

In contrast, DelBello had always desired a cordial relationship with the governor and had relished the opportunity to serve the residents of New York State. "I have no problem with Mario personally," he said. "I'm not sure whether it's him or the staff. Whatever it is, it's petty. There are no fundamental differences."

**With Mario Cuomo at St. Patrick's Day parade
in New York City.**

Even after leaving his post, he told the governor and the public, "I'll help him with any of his political campaigns." He came strongly to Cuomo's defense when state Comptroller Edward V. Regan falsely accused Cuomo of borrowing against future bud-gets to pay current bills.

"What we don't need is a comptroller... tearing down – improperly – the image of the state of New York fiscally," DelBello said.

After DelBello's departure, Cuomo was forced to endure two years of Republican Senate Majority Leader Anderson's service as lieutenant governor – a compulsory consequence of New York law. Cuomo was re-elected in 1986 with running mate Stanley Lundine, a smart, competent politician who had been mayor of Jamestown in western New York for six years before serving for a decade in Congress. Yet selecting a candidate from a municipality practically in the Midwest seemed a misstep for the governor – especially after Lundine himself had sided with the Koch-DelBello primary "ticket" in 1982. Many Democrats wanted to see Cuomo run for president in two years. Why Lundine and not anyone from more populous urban areas who could convincingly fill Cuomo's shoes?

Cuomo would claim that he chose Lundine because he wanted a lieutenant governor "who was competent to be governor immediately" – a clear slap at DelBello and a possible nod toward his own aspirations for higher office. The decision would come back to haunt him. Despite being pegged as a top contender in the 1988 presidential race, Cuomo spent months wringing his hands over whether to run, earning him the sobriquet "Hamlet on the Hudson." Ultimately, he decided against it, claiming that he couldn't leave New York with growing budget problems and challenges from the Repub-lican-dominated legislature. What he really might have been worried about was leaving his legacy in the hands of a relative unknown who would be knocked out in a re-election campaign.

Had Cuomo stuck with DelBello and even groomed him, he could have leapt onto the national stage knowing New York was in qualified, popular hands. His legacy would have been safe. Even if the state's economy ran onto the rocks – an unlikely outcome, given DelBello's fiscal integrity – Cuomo would have been shielded. DelBello would have taken the blame while Cuomo juggled world affairs. Instead, Cuomo drove him out of Albany. Now he would keep himself out of the White House.

By 1994, even Lundine was growing weary of Cuomo's equivocation. After he waffled for months on a fourth gubernatorial run, Lundine announced he would seek the Democratic nomination if Cuomo didn't. It was a word-for-word repetition of what Cuomo himself had said about Hugh Carey before pushing him aside in 1982. Cuomo, fearing a similar coup, took defensive measures. He flew to New York City for a meeting with his own financial backers, announcing his candidacy three days later. The ticket lost to Republican George Pataki.

What if DelBello had remained lieutenant governor? What if Cuomo had run for president? For that matter, what if President Bill Clinton had appointed Cuomo to the Supreme Court in 1993 instead of Ruth Bader Ginsburg? How might not only their careers but the fate of the state and the nation have been different?

Instead, DelBello's last official act as lieutenant governor was an exchange of political farewells in the same building where, nineteen years earlier, he had attended his first Yonkers City Council meeting as the newly elected councilman from the city's 10th Ward. It was his final meeting as chairman of the Yonkers Emergency Financial Control Board. At the end of the meeting, James Marrin, the control board's lawyer, read a two-page commendation humorously labeling DelBello "the Horatio Alger story of public life" and quite seriously as "an outstanding public servant."

After his return to Albany, DelBello met with the governor, who gave him a parting gift – a small statue of the Lady of Justice, scales held in balance and eyes blindfolded in judicial impartiality.

"It's the Lady of Justice," he said. "And the scales are fixed."

A photograph appeared in the newspaper, capturing the moment. It showed DelBello standing in front of Cuomo's desk, smiling over his gift with amusement and appreciation. Cuomo was seated behind his desk, scowling and gripping the armrests of his swivel chair as if he were ready to spring from his seat and usher in the end of the event. It was as revealing a photo as could have been taken, crystallizing the whole of their, at best, ambivalent political partnership.

Laughing with Republican State Senator Warren Anderson.

DelBello had a far more cordial reception as he returned to the State Senate on January 31 for his final legislative session. The packed audience of legislators greeted the Senate president with a standing ovation. Though a man of calm, understated emotion, DelBello was visibly moved when the session over which he was presiding turned into a forty-minute bipartisan tribute to his twenty-five-month tenure. He noted that in his twenty-year career, "nothing has been as crowning as being given the opportunity to preside over the Senate."

Senate Minor-ity Leader Manfred Ohrenstein said to him, "You are an extraordinary public servant who has articulated a vision of government with enormous clarity. You are probably one of the best managers that I have ever seen in government." Majority Leader Anderson, the lieutenant governor in waiting, hinted that DelBello might have replaced Cuomo if he had not chosen to resign.

"You had a great future in public service, not only in this chamber but elsewhere," Anderson offered. "Somebody said you're taking your gavel with you. You're welcome to it. You deserve it. You deserve more than that."

After lengthy applause and handshakes, DelBello walked to the front door of the Senate building. A steady snow swirled outside. He remembered an interview he had conducted recently in which he said why he was leaving his post in Albany.

"A new challenge, a new opportunity, a new career. Life's too short to do one thing," said the former lieutenant governor, county executive, mayor and councilman.

He breathed deep with resigned conviction and descended the marble steps of the Capitol building for the last time. Snowflakes clung to his black-rimmed glasses and dark overcoat. He strode toward his car as if walking into history, fading into sepia, a portrait of a leader among leaders, like the others honored in the City Hall of his beloved Yonkers.

CHAPTER FOUR

Beginnings, or
'What Have You Got to Lose?'

Nestled between the Bronx and Hudson Rivers from east to west, respectively, and the village of Hastings-on-Hudson and the boroughs of Manhattan and the Bronx north to south, Yonkers is a city of hills and waterways – geographic complements that mirror its historic diversity. Its name derives from *Jonkheer,* or *Jonker,* a title meaning "young lord" or "esquire" given to Adriaen van der Donck, a 16th-century Dutch landowner and lawyer in New York, then New Amsterdam, who tried to instill republican values in the hierarchical Dutch West India Company-run trading post.

It is urban and industrial, with all the challenges cities are heirs to. It is also a suburban vestige of Gilded Age glory and glamor, its riparian estates now home to such cultural attractions at the Hudson River Museum and the Untermyer Gardens Conservancy, along with such esteemed educational institutions as Sarah Lawrence College. In the past, Yonkers was known for crime, corruption, government inefficiency, and racial discrimination. Today it is a financial powerhouse, the third-largest city in New York State, one whose proximity to the Big Apple has made it a magnet for media companies like Lionsgate and a host of artists, including the singers Mary J. Blige and Ella Fitzgerald, who have claimed Yonkers as a hometown, a destination and a springboard to the wider world.

Yonkers' son

It was into this rich tapestry that DelBello was born on November 3, 1934, to Sylvester W. DelBello – a well-known attorney whose father, Gaetano, owned a bar and hotel on Main Street in Yonkers – and his wife, the former Marie Savio, a homemaker.

Public office had little appeal for the young Al, although events were already coalescing to lead him in that direction. At The Halsted School, a private, coeducational preparatory school on North Broadway in Yonkers, he excelled in sports and became a popular student known for his intellect and debating skills. Encouraged by the school's principal, he joined the student council and was quickly catapulted to president.

DelBello's father had run for the New York Supreme Court and, though unsuccessful, was active in community issues and served on the local board of education. DelBello had helped with his campaign and found both electioneering and community work compelling. He didn't give his own political aspirations much thought, though he had an affinity for public service. As a lawyer, he thought, he could hone the kind of reputation and networking skills that would make him a public hitching post in the center of town. In public life or private practice, that sort of exposure seemed practical.

In 1952, DelBello enrolled at Manhattan College, alma mater of his father and uncle, and went straight on to Fordham University for his law degree. He had already begun dating the woman who would become his wife, Dolores Rizzo, known as "Dee" at The College of New Rochelle, where she pursued a degree in fine arts with an eye to teaching.

They married immediately after he completed his law degree. The honeymoon would be brief as DelBello, enrolled in the National Guard throughout law school, was called into service. He reported to Fort Dix, New Jersey. After eight weeks of basic training, he was assigned to Fort Gordon, Georgia, a patchwork grid of military obeisance parked in the steaming southern reaches of red pine and tupelo, several miles from where the Savannah River carves a languorous, undulating border with South Carolina. The fort – named for Confederate Major General John Brown Gordon, who later in life became Georgia's governor – was the training base of General George S. Patton's Third Army. Nearly abandoned after World War II, the base quickly regained its military eminence as the training ground for the U.S. Army Signal Corps.

Fort Gordon itself was insular and functional, its heterogeneous culture not a far cry from New York's melting-pot sensibilities. In his Yonkers youth, DelBello had infrequently witnessed open racial discrimination, though, as with all parts of America, it was layered in the racial geology of the time. Discrimination up north was more territorial and more covert than hierarchical. Groups coalesced around neighborhoods and exerted pressure on one another through political allegiances. Discrimination varied by location, with competing strata for everyone to occupy.

Georgia's venomous hospitality was an eye-opener. Reconstruction had institutionalized slavery's less visible offenses, placing black citizens squarely in the crosshairs – and sometimes nooses – of a hateful white superstructure. Bigotry was endemic, lynching was frequent, and segregation was a fact of life so utterly ingrained in the southern worldview that its repugnance failed to generate even a political afterthought among most white citizens.

The atmosphere of egalitarianism in DelBello's military environs evaporated off the base. It shocked him when a group of his closest friends, including a young black man from Westchester County, were turned away at a movie box office because they refused to divide themselves into the theater's separate seating sections for blacks and whites. The experience molded him. For the first time in his life, he understood how a bigoted government could betray its own constitutional principles and fail the very people it served. Racism wasn't history. It was the most despicable moral failure of his day.

DelBello returned to Yonkers after six months in the National Guard, relieved to depart Georgia's cleaved culture. He settled into his father's law partnership in an office building just downhill from City Hall, amid a patchwork of industries, apartments, storefronts, churches and municipal institutions. Yonkers was infused with ethnic diversity and commerce. The downtown was packed with small businesses near a growing black community and the eponymously named Italian Park Hill neighborhood.

The work at his father's firm forged DelBello's relationships with Yonkers' residents, but he found it dull. His father's clients were hesitant to trust their lawyer's son, which saddled DelBello with tedious cases. He needed something more meaningful. He opened a practice with another young attorney, where he built his own list of clients and established his identity as a local leader in law and commerce.

A politician is born

Four years later, after moving to a new home in Yonkers' 10th Ward, DelBello was asked by Democratic Party ward leader Al Noonan – also the Yonkers public works commissioner – if he would be interested in running for 10th Ward councilman in the 1963 election. The Yonkers Common Council – the city's mercurial legislature – seemed like a good opportunity for the young lawyer, one sure to boost his connections.

DelBello was surprised by Noonan's interest. He had been marginally involved in political issues for several years and was a new resident of the 10th Ward. Noonan asked him to run against the powerful Andrew Hayduk, a Republican icon first elected to public office in the 1930s. Andrew and his brother Albert – the Yonkers Republican city chairman – were considered among the most influential men in town. It seemed like a losing proposition, but a great opportunity to spar with the big boys and get his feet wet. DelBello accepted.

He conducted an intensive campaign, knocking on virtually every door in the 10th Ward and handing out mimeographed flyers. His persistence paid off. He came remarkably close to defeating the entrenched Hayduk, a political rout by Yonkers measures. Two years later, in 1965, when DelBello proposed a second run, Noonan refused to give him the nod. DelBello was incredulous. Why would the Democratic ward leader suddenly reverse himself, especially after his near-victorious run the last time around?

Furious with Noonan's dismissal, DelBello threatened to sue him over the party's procedures – and to run in a Democratic primary campaign against any challenger. Noonan didn't want a family squabble on his watch. Thinking that his powerful buddy and Republican fixer Andy Hayduck would win anyway, he grudgingly endorsed DelBello. Primed for a fight, he ran a blistering campaign against Hayduk and won. The young lawyer who had just celebrated his thirty-first birthday beat the unbeatable longtime Republican incumbent and political insider. His upset victory was so improbable that the Republican-leaning Herald Statesman headlined "Hayduk Loses" on its front page. It was the beginning of a political legacy.

DelBello was one of only two Democrats on the twelve-member city council. The remainder of the council and the mayor were Republicans, though certainly not patsies of the party's celebrated governor, Nelson A. Rockefeller. In Yonkers, loyalty to local politics came first. Occupying a diminutive Democratic space, DelBello would need the cooperation of his Republican brethren.

That test of interparty camaraderie came quickly when Rockefeller used his state power to acquire a large, serene parcel of land adjacent to the 10th Ward's Homefield neighborhood – one that contained an aging hospital – for use as a heroin-addiction rehabilitation center. This proposal had followed several years of suspicious zoning changes that dramatically increased the value of the land – enough to make a state acquisition highly desirable to the owners.

The treatment center would not only bring New York City addicts to a relatively unsecured site in the middle of Yonkers but also would result in the loss of more than a half-million dollars in annual real estate tax revenue once the site became state property. Citizens were up in arms, and several Republican councilmen joined in. Little warning was given regarding the state's move. Even former Yonkers Mayor and State Senator John Flynn, a Republican, was caught off guard and given only twenty-four hours to rally public opposition.

'What have you got to lose?'

DelBello wasn't opposed to the idea of drug addiction treatment. Indeed, he strongly backed the idea of a treatment facility on the unused Fort Slocum site, located on a small island just off New Rochelle's coast, where security would be substantial, and community real estate values would remain unaffected. He quickly garnered the support of citizens and the backing of a number of Republican politicians, including Flynn, all of whom felt betrayed by the state's lightning move. After helping organize a 500-person protest at City Hall, citizens staged a weeks-long occupation of an access bridge to the site. DelBello became the movement's leader.

Lieutenant Governor (Charles) Malcolm Wilson – himself a Yonkers native – claimed that he was "ashamed" by the opposition to a treatment center. He publicly rebuked DelBello as a "peanut politician." It was a golden moment. With a keen sense of marketing – and humor – DelBello suggested that the opposition group call itself the "Peanut Citizens' Committee." It was a prescient moniker for the hundreds of citizens who joined the committee. Throughout his many efforts, DelBello was able to gain enormous support from the regular folks in Yonkers. Unlike today's computer age, DelBello's power of communication and leadership came from the people who supported and believed in him. It was "people power."

The Peanut Citizens' Committee became the political fulcrum for growing voter dissatisfaction with other persistent governmental shortcomings. The Yonkers Record penned an editorial praising the young DelBello as a trailblazer. The paper took unwavering aim at both the governor and those Republican councilmen who supported Rockefeller's land coup, urging voters to boot them out in the next election. The efforts to stop the treatment center were ultimately unsuccessful, but DelBello had clearly established himself as an advocate for Yonkers' voters.

Although his public prestige had blossomed, he discovered he had little influence over city management. DelBello was a man with a moral compass on a council that had for decades been dominated by corruption, ineptitude and political influence peddling. Contracts were awarded to favored friends. Building inspectors took bribes to endorse lucrative zoning changes. The city budget had run at a deficit for ten years. Bad public service was shrugged off as the way of ward politics – culminating in a public works fiasco during 1969's historic blizzard, which crippled the city for days.

The mayor at the time, James F.X. O'Rourke, M.D. – an eye surgeon whose unusual career trajectory took him from singing and football to politics – had tried to push through reforms to tamp down corruption, but his own influence was limited. The city manager, charged with administering public employees and programs, reported to the council rather than the mayor. Although the city manager often advocated the mayor's plans and positions, the council could run interference on pet projects.

Patronage for city jobs was endemic, and city managers were often pressured to hire poorly qualified friends and family of council members to head important city departments. Managers who resisted soon found themselves on the unemployment line. Yonkers tore through six city managers in six years. O'Rourke tried to end this cycle by persuading the Republican majority on the council to hire a professional city manager, the first one in two decades. Ten months later, that manager quit in frustration.

Despite the successful work DelBello had done in his four years as a two-term councilman, he was becoming disenchanted by the city's political inertia, wayward corruption, and persistent debt. One night, after a long and frustrating council meeting, he arrived home and told Dee that he planned to drop out of the next council race. He had known when he first ran for councilman that Yonkers politics was something of a free-for-all, but he thought he would have been able to do more to transform government – to make it more professional, more responsive to the voters who had elected him. He was demoralized.

"It's hopeless," he told Dee. "Corruption is running wild, and I'm thinking about not running for re-election next year."

"Well, then why not run for mayor?" she said. "If you win, you can do something about it. If not, you're off the council anyway. What have you got to lose?"

CHAPTER FIVE

The Clean-Up Hitter

DelBello's opponent in the mayor's race, Republican James F.X. O'Rourke, M.D., was an ophthalmologist and Yonkers city councilman who had been appointed mayor by Governor Nelson A. Rockefeller after the December 1966 departure of John Flynn to the State Senate. O'Rourke was an honest, ethical man steeped in the Irish-Catholic tradition. A handsome figure with a mellifluous voice, he was a husband and father of thirteen children, a man who had briefly played professional football before serving in the army in World War II, where he earned a Purple Heart while leading his platoon to capture a German town. (In this, DelBello would later see personal, though not political, parallels with New York State Governor Hugh Carey.) O'Rourke, then, was the perfect candidate.

Like the ancient Greek heroes, however, he had a fatal flaw: He knew that corruption was a cancer on his beloved Yonkers, and he was powerless to stop it.

Political patronage had been the ethos of Yonkers for decades – a nostalgic relic that was now corroding. City problems had become bigger than the deceased statesmen whose images graced the corridors of City Hall could ever have imagined. Neighborhood issues may have still been the crucible of local politics, but the landscape of the late-20th century was teeming with commerce and culture, health care and housing issues, educational and infrastructure challenges, and many new residents, all sweeping north from New York City. For these multifaceted times, citizens demanded more responsible public management than the myopic days of patronage could provide.

O'Rourke had won re-election in 1967 by a precariously small margin. Voters were impatient but not yet outraged. He pushed to change the council's powerful patronage machine but was resisted at every turn by his own Republican majority. With few other options, the good doctor had called upon Rockefeller to appoint the State Investigation Commission (SIC) to treat the city's chronic ailments of bribery and fraud.

It was the right therapy, but a costly one. Unable to distance himself adequately from his Republican brethren on the council, O'Rourke took the brunt of voter outrage over shady insider deals and managerial incompetence. Though grateful for his help in exposing city cronyism, DelBello felt he hadn't gone far enough and used the never-ending corruption in Yonkers against him. It hurt O'Rourke in the debates and ultimately cost him his job.

A prediction comes true

DelBello was elected with a stunning majority in November 1969 – an election the right-leaning local journals had hoped he would lose. The thirty-five-year-old Democrat was the youngest mayor-elect in Yonkers' history. Against the backdrop of an older, deeply entrenched Republican council and mayor, his ascendancy was a clear mandate for change.

It was a surprise for DelBello. While in his formative years, he had participated on the debating team and had become president of the student council at Halsted; he had brushed off the idea of a career in politics. Now, as he was swarmed by well-wishers and reporters, he recalled his high school English teacher, Mrs. Monroe, saying in a crisp English accent, "I believe you will be the mayor of Yonkers someday, Alfred."

DelBello had been elected in a schizophrenic year of crisis and achievement that careened between wrenching TV news scenes of wounded American soldiers being airlifted from sweltering Vietnam battlefields to the first grainy, black-and-white images of human beings standing on the moon. The Woodstock concert – which took place about 100 miles northwest of Yonkers in Bethel – celebrated the "summer of love" while race riots and angry anti-war protests fanned flames at family dinner tables across the country.

By the time he took the oath of office on January 1, 1970, the city's corruption and favoritism had become mind-boggling. The infamous snowplow fiasco during the winter of 1969 had cost Yonkers $650,000. An additional $1 million had been spent on renting a fleet of garbage trucks to cart municipal trash twenty miles to dump it in the Croton Point Landfill. Yonkers got stuck with Croton's $8.30-per-ton cost for transportation and dumping, while mob-controlled private carriers shelled out less than $1 per ton at the city's own incinerator.

Meanwhile, pricey local contractors, many unqualified and tied to organized crime, lined their pockets as the city racked up $12 million in debt in less than a decade. Robberies were common, illegal drugs were endemic, and violent crime was on the rise.

In the smoldering rubble of a political earthquake, Yonkers voters – finally exhausted by the graft, greed and inertia of their own leaders – pegged their hopes on a vibrant young upstart of a mayor. DelBello capitalized on the public's demand for responsible leadership, moving quickly to enact a panoply of sorely needed changes.

The battle lines had actually been drawn right before he became mayor. The city council's last official act of 1969, days before his inauguration, was to refuse to consider the revised proposed 1970 budget, which included salary increases for police, firefighters and teachers. The budget, negotiated during the previous administration, needed to be ratified by the council. By refusing to pass it, the budget would have to be resubmitted to the new council after January 1. That would make it look as if the budget and expected tax increases had been all DelBello's doing. It would also force public employees to work without a contract for at least a week or more, possibly resulting in strikes. It was political theater at its most unfair.

DelBello lambasted the outgoing mayor and the council, calling it one of "the most irresponsible acts I've ever seen." Responding to comments from Republican council members that he was about to break his promise not to raise taxes, he retorted, "Anyone with half a brain can see that the taxes are paying off the deficit the Republicans have accumulated over the past two years."

The professional

This was precisely the kind of insider bickering that convinced DelBello to seek staff from outside of Yonkers. Hiring topnotch professionals was the only way to create meaningful change. He had insisted that the council support his choices to head each department. He started with the tough, intractable Seymour Scher as his city manager, his first and most important hire. He had brought him in after his long and successful stint as city manager in Rochester. DelBello knew Scher was exactly the kind of principled fighter he needed to help him clean up Yonkers. He was honest, highly professional and didn't take kindly to threats or bullying. Scher was the tip of the spear in DelBello's armament to professionalize city government.

The appointment of someone with Scher's credentials was pivotal in ridding the Yonkers government of corruption and sloth. Since by Yonkers' charter, the city manager and other department commissioners reported to the council, the mayor was essentially a defanged executive and 13th councilman-at-large. The council could pressure a manager to acquiesce or face termination. This absence of managerial reliability, paired with top-level department corruption, meant that the city would meander, year after year, through incompetence and financial ruin.

DelBello had corrected that by demanding that the city manager as well as the top three positions in any department were his and his alone to fill. His aggressive approach hinged on his relationships with council members. Having served two terms as 10th Ward councilman prior to his ascendance, he understood the demands of the local legislature. Party politics had always played second fiddle to power. He negotiated with the council. "Just give me this," he said. "And things will be better for you. Your constituents want Yonkers to succeed."

The council acceded to his request for recruiting flexibility. DelBello went on to hire from a nationwide list of top government professionals, including Raymond Miller, a retired army colonel from Virginia. Miller took charge as commissioner of the Department of Public Works, the agency that had failed so spectacularly in the 1969 blizzard. Miller had served as chief engineer for the United States Continental Army Command. Tough, direct and methodical, the commissioner, whose staff referred to him as "the Colonel," cleared his carpeted office, arranging it as a fully staffed, twenty-four-hour command post to deal with complaints about snow removal, floods and other less dramatic problems.

'The Big Six'

But DelBello knew that solving the city's problems required going beyond his own jurisdiction. Even before he took the oath of office, he assembled a team of mayors from New York's other large cities to draw statewide attention to shared urban problems. Dubbed "The Big Six," this new coalition of mayors from New York City, Albany, Buffalo, Syracuse and Rochester would help him increase his influence with the state legislature in Albany.

In DelBello's first month as mayor, he organized a bus tour for the mayors, with himself as the guide, to highlight decaying residential properties, high-crime areas, potholes and closed businesses. He didn't try to show off the sunny side of Yonkers, but rather exposed problems he knew plagued the other mayors as well. His laments about the state's acquisition of taxable land for highways – and the controversial Ridge Hill narcotics treatment hospital – reverberated.

The other mayors relayed their war stories of rising crime, drugs and corporate flight. New York City Mayor John Lindsay, the handsome, affable Republican who would soon turn Democrat, bonded with DelBello. They discussed common problems, some of which bled across their shared border. Teaming up with other mayors was a brilliant power play.

State legislators were now being petitioned by a unified urban front with a shared agenda, rather than individual mayors with hats in hand. It began to transform the dynamics in Albany. In just weeks, DelBello had made New York's top mayors a bipartisan tactical team on the political field of battle.

The Big Six fought for "revenue-sharing," a new approach to state and possibly federal funding in which a specific portion of taxes collected from their cities would be earmarked for their unique challenges – housing, redevelopment, emergency services and other essential aid. An enormous percentage of state revenues came from the cities. Why should all the money go into general funds? DelBello hoped the team could convince the state legislature to establish the revenue-sharing program.

Touring Yonkers with the "Big Six" mayors. From left: Buffalo Mayor Frank Sedito, New York City Mayor John Lindsay, Yonkers Mayor Alfred Del Bello, and Syracuse Mayor Lee Alexander.

It was no small financial matter. The mayors were seeking close to $1 billion in aid. They wanted the state to take over public school funding in their cities, pay their local shares of welfare costs, help fund police – especially in light of Rockefeller's own antidrug mandates – and compensate them for lost revenue from state-acquired city properties, like Ridge Hill. Welfare and subsidized housing were a tremendous burden for the mayors. Though they supported state and federal mandates for these things, they often lost money because the financial burden was so much greater than the small revenue these programs produced. They needed more state and federal financial support.

Rockefeller was sympathetic. He liked the idea, but he told them flatly that the price tag was too high. Expect less funding, he said. Yet months later, they had won a twenty-one percent revenue-sharing deal from the state and a restoration of prior cuts in educational funding. It was a decisive victory.

Yonkers was still walking a financial tightrope, but these funding assurances meant DelBello could move ahead with badly needed changes for the police, firefighters and other emergency services. He needed new patrol cars, supplies and even street lighting for public parks and high-crime areas. Yonkers faced a tough crime problem, but its 490 officers were sufficient to do the job when properly funded. He was concerned about morale, however. The city's prior leadership had ignored increasing crimes and the underlying problems that caused it – the housing shortage, high rents, declining business opportunities, inadequate drug treatment and particularly a troubled school system.

School daze

Perhaps nothing bothered DelBello, who had been fortunate enough to attend the private Halsted School, more than the persistent disregard for the well-being and education of children. Several public schools, like the Emerson School (now the Cross Hill Academy and Yonkers Early Childhood Academy), were models of learning. But other public schools were a disgrace. The now-defunct Longfellow Junior High School, home to predominantly low-income minority students, was in appalling disrepair. At the invitation of the staff, DelBello toured the school. The physical conditions were inexcusable – poor heating and ventilation, dangerous exits and broken doors that offered easy access to drug addicts and criminals. Still, the teachers were good, and they loved their students. It offended DelBello that a Yonkers public school could be in such a condition and that its children could be so egregiously neglected. "It's a disgrace," he said.

The next week, at DelBello's urging, the children and a few of the teachers from Longfellow showed up at the city council meeting to demand better conditions. They asked the council

With then-Senator Joe Biden.

members to tour the school themselves – as the mayor just had. DelBello was thrilled. They had begun to take action on their own, all because a mayor finally cared about them. He would be able to do something about it as well. Because of the city's daunting deficit, school upgrades had been placed on hold. But DelBello had been able to cut city spending and refinance the deficit. Now, with an additional $4.5 million that he had procured from the federal government, sorely needed repairs, increased security, classrooms and a library were added to Longfellow and another existing school, and construction began on a new high school to meet student needs.

Safe schools were merely the beginning of DelBello's plan for supporting Yonkers' youth. Realizing the importance of after-school and summer jobs in keeping children away from crime and drug use, he started the city's Rent-a-Kid program for after-school employment. He established the HEY (Help Employ Youth) summertime jobs initiative and, with federal funding, turned it into the fully staffed Cooperative Area Manpower Planning System (CAMPS). These programs complemented the city's broad-based Community Action Program, an overarching initiative to help poor communities avoid crime, find housing, access health services and provide a student-to-student science mentorship program.

For kids already in trouble, DelBello established the Youth Services Agency (YSA), which worked to prevent juvenile delinquency and drug abuse through halfway houses and community centers. The program became the first fully staffed agency of its type in New York State. The YSA worked hand in hand with the Renaissance Program – a drug counseling and recovery agency long advocated by DelBello as a better alternative to the problematic and expensive Ridge Hill narcotics facility that Rockefeller had planted in Yonkers over the objections of citizens.

All of these programs helped financially disadvantaged

children and adults lead more productive lives. The vast majority of its beneficiaries were people of color, many of Puerto Rican descent. These programs were not bromides for which many other liberal-leaning white politicians had dutifully advocated. DelBello had long believed that America's history of discrimination against people of color demanded more than feel-good programs. He wanted basic fairness and opportunity for minority communities. He reflected on his shock at discovering the severity of America's ingrained racism when he had served in the National Guard in Georgia. Within the year, DelBello had earned the James J. Hoey Award for Interracial Justice presented by the Catholic Interracial Council of New York. The award was a nice tribute. But the work of equalizing opportunity for children, its own reward, was just beginning.

He was also moved to help children – and their primary caregivers, mothers – early in their lives. In 1971, he opened Yonkers' first daycare center, a long-overdue facility that would help working women and their families take care of their preschool children. He established the Day Care Coordinating Council to make sure that the government carried the flag for working women. By summertime, DelBello had also petitioned federal legislators to endorse the Child Development Act, which would provide the city with $500,000 in daycare funding. "Daycare centers are needed on all economic levels. It's not purely a poor problem," he said, predicting the rising role of women in the workplace.

Gimme shelter

DelBello had put in place a host of programs that had never existed to deal with crime, drug addition, youth jobs and school funding. He had leveraged millions of dollars from both the state and federal governments. But the paucity of housing helped poverty persist. Throughout the city, rising rental prices were still at crisis levels. A river of complaints had flowed into City Hall. Landlords were jacking up rents without control because of the short supply of apartments, even though services in the buildings – like heat and water – continued to decline. Even public housing tenants were paying more than double their rent from several years earlier as living conditions declined. DelBello had worked with the state legislature to pass two bipartisan rent control bills giving Yonkers home-rule rent guideline powers. Rockefeller vetoed both. It was maddening.

But the city government, prior to DelBello's administration, had been just as much to blame. Millions of dollars had been available over many years to build affordable housing for Yonkers' citizens. But little of that money had been tapped by O'Rourke and the city council. In the previous twenty-one years, the city had obtained only $1.9 million in federal funding and built only a single publicly funded housing project – just one in two decades while cities like White Plains had received $39 million in federal funding and Rochester close to $100 million. DelBello considered this an act of political negligence.

That was about to change. In his first term, DelBello obtained $13 million in urban renewal aid for slum clearance – over six times as much as in the previous two decades combined. He created 1,900 new housing units and programmed 1,200 more per year. The rate at which new apartments were being created was unprecedented. Perhaps more important, he instituted tenants' rights as a city government responsibility through a new rent control department. The office, created through a cooperative effort with county and state government, provided public information and established a hearing process so that tenants and landlords could mediate disagreements.

"Yonkers has the major rent control population in the county," he said, "and it should have a convenient facility" for mediating disagreements.

DelBello traveled to Albany to push legislators for the right of tenants to strike. Democratic and even some Republican legislators were aghast when Angelo Martinelli, the businessman who would oppose him in the 1971 mayoral race, tried to convince them that DelBello had failed to do anything about housing in Yonkers. Most legislators didn't buy it.

But the tenants' council of the Municipal Housing Authority (MHA) did. The tenants had pressed DelBello to do more. They were unhappy with the lack of progress during his first term – the crime, drugs and poor housing conditions – though they acknowledged that no progress had been made in prior years either. So why their dissatisfaction with DelBello, especially when he was clearly making progress on local and state regulations to protect renters?

Perhaps they were spurred on by Martinelli, who had placed the absence of rent control in DelBello's lap, despite the fact that his own party leader, Governor Nelson Rockefeller, had twice vetoed the state rent control legislation that DelBello had pushed among his party's legislators.

Although rent control legislation was stalled in Albany, he pressed on with his urban agenda. The new, affordable units coming online raised the interest of commercial real estate investors. With cheaper, better and more abundant living units now available to citizens who had barely been able to pay their rents, there would be more dollars in people's wallets. But so much of Yonkers, especially the downtown, was outdated and needed a complete overhaul. On this matter, real estate developers, building owners and tenants could all agree.

A land-use plan paired with desperately needed public infrastructure was the only thing that could stimulate large private investment in real estate. Commercial property improvements depended on new streets, rebuilt sidewalks and public spaces to make Yonkers a commercial destination. Getty Square, the jewel in the city's rough, became the focus of redevelopment. DelBello would hire famed architect I.M. Pei, the man who would add a modern pyramid to Paris' Musée du Louvre, to build the new Yonkers Civic Center and a pedestrian bridge connecting the court buildings and City Hall into one large plaza.

Getting people to Getty Square, though, was still a problem. While revitalization plans moved forward, the Nepperhan Avenue artery needed significant upgrades so that Getty Square businesses would be accessible by cars and pedestrians. State funding was tight, and the Department of Transportation was stalling. The first phase of the arterial upgrade hinged on $3 million in state funding to assemble commercial parcels so the avenue could be widened. Now DelBello and City Manager Scher were being told by the DOT that funding austerity had curtailed their plans. A start date was uncertain. More than $60 million in commercial investment was on hold. With the help of State Senator John Flynn, however, the money was finally released just days before the 1971 election.

Environmental advocate

All urban politicians seek government-funded economic development projects like Getty Square that can boost urban life. But big projects are often sought at the expense of small ones that strengthen the city's fabric. Neighborhood-scale projects, like cleaning parks, installing walkways and painting murals on buildings, can make the biggest difference in the lives of average citizens. And they happen quickly. It might take years to rebuild a road or civic center, but only a week to beautify a park. These smaller projects also get people directly involved in fixing their own neighborhoods, usually working as volunteers with small sources of local funds supported by donations from local businesses that wanted to see rapid changes on their own city blocks. Neighborhoods were where the political rubber met the road.

DelBello inspired volunteers and schoolchildren to improve their neighborhoods in these small but pivotal ways. He established the Neighborhood Improvement Program, where volunteer citizens and school kids would coordinate with various city agencies to paint murals, create "alley" parks and clean public spaces. Again, using more than $100,000 in federal funds he had secured, he hired architects from New York City to draw up plans for better public spaces and local contractors to improve park facilities.

He turned the dilapidated John F. Kennedy Marina into a temporary outdoor musical venue while plans were being developed for more extensive site improvements. Thousands crowded the marina for the American Waterways Wind Orchestra, a part of the Centennial Summer Festival of the Arts DelBello had arranged. Sculpture contests were held, walls were painted, and benches and tables were installed. Small spaces and pathways throughout the city, long seen by its own residents as dangerous, overgrown eyesores, were now coming alive with art, landscaping and, most important, people – who once again took pride in the city and believed in its future. It was clearly a more desirable alternative to candidate Martinelli's proposal – using state funds to create a 170-acre landfill on the edge of the Hudson, a disposal concept that would soon dominate Westchester politics in the upriver town of Croton-on-Hudson, home of the Croton Point Landfill.

An avid environmentalist long before the term was popularized, DelBello also solicited the involvement of citizens by organizing urban cleanups. Open spaces such as the Hollow, a memorial parkland along the Saw Mill River Parkway, received $161,000 in state money as a result of his environmental advocacy. He obtained more than $1 million in federal funding for the city's open space programs in his first two years alone.

With the advent of the first Earth Day in 1970, the issue of air pollution and its ominous impact on the health of residents was of paramount importance. DelBello established the first citywide health council and the Mayor's Environmental Committee for Action to study pollution and propose bottle recycling legislation. He installed fly-ash control technology at the city incinerator to clamp down on air emissions – foreshadowing the role waste management would play in his tenure as Westchester County executive.

DelBello knew that no matter how big the initiatives he pursued and how high he climbed as a leader, local action would always be what made a difference in the lives of voters and earned him their trust. While he fought for large projects, like affordable apartment buildings, he understood that these ground-up initiatives based on self-reliance and citizen involvement did the most to drive redevelopment policy. He was leading his constituents to lead themselves.

Perhaps most important to voters, he did something that, by modern standards, sounds like a political platitude. He actually fixed City Hall. He established the first personnel office – a stunning void in governmental management that had gone on for far too long. He saved millions of dollars eliminating political patronage jobs without cutting needed civil personnel. He even created new programs and positions that had been financially crowded out by the previous governmental waste. And he filed a series of lawsuits to recover some of the misappropriated funds from the prior administration.

DelBello strengthened his emphasis on consumer issues and civic life, establishing a first-of-its-kind Citizens Service Center to help with many problems that might fall outside more conventional offices. Citizens could call the office to find a reliable plumber, a practice space for a rock band or mental health assistance for a family member. At a time before the internet, the center was a helpful, live alternative to hunting down numbers in the phone book.

In an act driven as much by his personal experience as his policy, he created the first student senate to interact with City Hall. Students met with city officials once a month to provide input on pressing urban issues. DelBello remembered his teenage years at The Halsted School when he served as student president. He remembered how one of his teachers, Mrs. Monroe, had predicted that he would be the mayor of Yonkers someday. As he greeted visiting students, he couldn't help but wonder if a future Yonkers mayor was standing among them.

Reaching out

DelBello also connected with citizens in other ways. He began hosting a regular Sunday evening radio show on WFAS-FM, with a call-in feature for listeners so he could answer the public directly.

"I'm a husband, father and attorney, in addition to being the mayor of Yonkers," he said. "The problems that worry each of the people are the same ones that worry me at home and at the office. It's time we get together and discuss them."

Nothing, though, bespoke his personal commitment to his community more than his nighttime visits with city residents.

He and his wife Dee would occasionally stay overnight in underserved homes with the people who lived there. A news crew would follow him and air the stories. He would talk with his hosts about problems such as crime, poverty, poor transportation – and rats, lots of rats. It was an issue as emblematic as any. Rats infested poor tenements and rich neighborhoods alike. The city's walled-off wards had become like a collection of feudal states fighting over food. The rats had become the city's unintended equalizer, feasting on the scraps of political battle.

DelBello dispatched them with a citywide eradication program – proving he was indeed Yonkers' Pied Piper.

CHAPTER SIX

Garbage, Guns, and Guts

Among the first calls Mayor DelBello had placed after his 1969 election was a courtesy call to Robert Morganthau, U.S. attorney for the Southern District of New York. Morganthau responded as if he had been expecting to hear from the reform-minded mayor. The hearings of the State Investigation Committee (SIC) were in progress, and DelBello wanted to discuss how his administration could begin to transform the corrupt political system in Yonkers. Morganthau asked Del-Bello if he could meet with him and the head of the FBI for the New York region. DelBello was a bit surprised. He had run on a platform of cleaning up city government but hadn't expected such interest from the district attorney.

They met several days later. Morganthau wanted to make DelBello fully aware of the severity of crime and political graft in Yonkers, particularly the people he should avoid. Morganthau knew things that DelBello didn't, at least not in the painfully exquisite detail in which some of the city's corruption was gradually coming to light – the sheer incompetence and fraud within the Department of Public Works, insider pocket padding, prearranged purchasing to reward favored friends and, perhaps most unconscionable, mob control of the city's sanitation business. There were players who would revel in DelBello's undoing. Morganthau wanted him to know where the landmines were being buried. He knew that cleaning up Yonkers would take more than two years and that the road to re-election would be treacherous. He needed DelBello to make it through his first term intact. It wouldn't be easy.

Trash talk

Years before his 1969 election, the Yonkers' city council had obediently acquiesced to the area's private carting services for commercial garbage pickups. The trash trucks were run by one of the region's most powerful organized crime syndicates. The mob had cornered the market on commercial collections and assumed exclusive control of the city's only public incinerator. Over time, it had muscled the city to drive down tipping fees – which were based on the weight of the waste to be disposed of – flooding the facility with its own trash and effectively barring entry to city trash trucks.

Public carters had to lumber more than twenty miles to the Croton Point Landfill to dump residential refuse at great expense to taxpayers, while private, crime-controlled carriers had the luxury of local disposal at rock-bottom rates.

The garbage czar of Yonkers and indeed the entire county was Nicholas A. "Cockeyed Nick" Rattenni, who owned more than ninety percent of the city's private collection business. With a lengthy arrest record but only one conviction dating back forty years, Rattenni had spent a quarter-century building a lucrative Westchester trash empire, using guile, insider deals and payola as his primary means of investment. He housed himself and his two daughters on a twelve-acre Yonkers estate, complete with a driving range, putting green and three stately homes, as well as a three-bedroom "playhouse" more stylish than the dwellings of many hard-working Yonkers natives.

Going up against Rattenni was a tough task for anyone, much less the city's first Italian-American mayor, whose surname fed the cultural bias of the time – that he himself was associated with the mob. At the end of the 1960s, Yonkers, and indeed much of America, was a nation of distinct cultures, ethnic neighborhoods – and prejudices. Al and Dee remembered hosting a reception at their home while he was mayor. A small group of up-county party leaders exploring his ambitions for county executive was apprehensive of how a Yonkers Italian would fare as a countywide candidate on the driving ranges and clay courts of Bedford and Scarsdale.

"Hmm, linen napkins," a bee-hived, blue-eyed socialite chirped in saccharine disdain at the buffet table, feigning pleasant surprise at the absence of chrome-plated paper napkin dispensers typical of Italian pizza parlors. It was a white-gloved indignity that irked the young mayor. But DelBello's clash with Rattenni didn't spring from any need to defend his heritage or prove his integrity. It was simply the right thing to do.

Garbage was the king of criminal enterprises in Yonkers, but only one part of a far-reaching pattern of endemic corruption. The winter before DelBello's election, when the deeply frustrated 10th Ward councilman started his campaign for mayor, the region had endured an epic blizzard. The city's response was one of devastating mismanagement and incompetence. As Milton Hoffman detailed in the Herald Statesman's "Grand Jury Probers Cite Mismanagement" (July 7, 1970), a dearth of snowplows and an ersatz management plan had left the city woefully unprepared. There was no advance salting, no preemptive parking restrictions, and no coordinated citywide response. Plow blades had not even been attached to the few trucks that were available for service.

Twenty inches of gale-driven snow sculpted six-foot drifts in the streets. The incredulously named Department of Public Works was notably absent. City employees frantically thumbed the Yellow Pages to hire private plows. Individual councilmen telephoned contractor friends to remove snow only in their own wards to placate their constituents. Plow trucks were stuck behind buried cars. It was a fiasco.

It was later revealed that fraud had been as widespread as incompetence. One contractor, the father of the acting city manager at that time, was credited with frugality, having billed City Hall only $530 for several twenty-hour days of work. But the dates on his invoices raised eyebrows: There was no February 29 that year. And – much to the amusement of the grand jury that subsequently investigated the city – there had never been a February 30. This "holiday-on-vice" had cost taxpayers an estimated $650,000. Bills had been paid by unauthorized city officials with no records of work done weeks after the storm had passed. Invoices were poorly recorded or missing entirely. Six Yonkers contractors were indicted for overcharging the city. The findings would have been laughable had they not been so appalling.

In March 1971, the State Investigation Committee released its report, a scathing indictment of the local corruption that had preceded DelBello's mayoral ascension. Morganthau had built several important indictments against local officials – one of them a council member. During DelBello's brief time in office, he had wrested control of garbage collection and disposal. The tipping point came when the private carters jacked up collection rates by fifteen percent, leaving local merchants in the lurch. The mob had overplayed its hand.

DelBello swept in emergency legislation allowing "hardship" collections and pressed the city council to authorize city-run commercial pickups at much lower rates.

The city once again had full access to its own incinerator. It had begun out-competing the carting barons for commercial trash pickups and forcing them to pay market-rate disposal fees at the city facility. It was one of many feathers in Del-Bello's cap. Less than two years into his first term as mayor, DelBello had crippled graft, fixed flawed emergency response systems, filled top agency seats with nationally recognized professionals and turned around the city's finances. The budget was in the black, a triumphant political punctuation ending a decade of deficits.

The bullet-proof candidate

Just weeks before the city's elections, DelBello was in his office preparing for a meeting with the city council when his receptionist knocked on his door. She was nervous.

"Mayor DelBello, it's the police. They want to see you."

DelBello looked up from his desk, furrowing his brow behind his black, thick-framed glasses.

"Yes, show them in right away."

The commander of the Yonkers police, William F. Polsen, and his assistant entered the office. They removed their hats. DelBello offered them a seat. They politely refused and remained standing.

"Mr. Mayor, your campaign headquarters was shot up yesterday. There are no injuries or anything like that, just bullets from what we think were two different handguns. It happened late last night. Also," Polsen paused, then glanced at his partner. "A load of garbage was dumped on Sy Scher's lawn. Same guys, I presume."

Though taken aback, DelBello had to resist the urge to smile, knowing how tough-minded and unintimidated Scher was. The police assigned DelBello and his wife Dee a security detail. But the assault on his campaign office and Scher's lawn only emboldened him, he later recalled: "To make those kinds of threats was pretty stupid. It didn't deter anything."

Tenants' strike

Mob threats weren't DelBello's only challenge in an election year. His opponent repeatedly claimed that the mayor's bipartisan efforts were just a foil to get re-elected. Martinelli railed against "unkept promises," even though DelBello hadn't yet completed his first term. He called the mayor insensitive. He blamed Scher for disregarding the issues that mattered to the average citizen. And he once again placed the failure of Yonkers' rent control bill – vetoed by his own party's Republican governor – squarely in DelBello's lap.

Allied with Martinelli, the Tenants' Council of the Municipal Housing Authority (MHA) staged a rent strike. But DelBello himself had stated publicly that a rent strike would be justified. Yet it also frustrated him. Time and time again, he had been stymied in his own efforts to create rent control, tenant strike protection and a tenant-landlord court by the Republican governor and Republican state legislators. All of them had resisted change for years, fearing pressure from the real estate industry. Now – with an election on the horizon – Martinelli was claiming that DelBello was the one blocking progress.

On September 30, 1971, with only five weeks until the election, a local newspaper, the Yonkers Record, dropped a political bombshell with the headline "Martinelli is Slum Breeder." A front-page photograph showed a burned-out building in the downtown business district that had never been rehabilitated. The structure was an eyesore and apparently a breeding ground for rats. Martinelli was the owner.

The story revealed it had been in disrepair since 1967. Martinelli had repeatedly been summoned to court to fix or demolish the abandoned building. He never did. Neighboring building owners and tenants were furious about the blight. The city's courts were on his case. Suddenly, Martinelli's reputation as the city's champion for affordable housing was dwindling.

But the MHA Tenants' Council supported him in the November election. What most citizens saw on the ground, however, after two years of DelBello's mayoral leadership was undeniable – clean streets, rehabilitated parks, new shops and restaurants, mounting real estate investments, local rent stabilization, and a feeling of pride they had thought had all but disappeared from Yonkers life. The budget was balanced. Corruption had been banished from City Hall. Crime was down. Business was up. Yonkers was back.

DelBello had ridden into the mayor's office in 1969 on the promise of change. He delivered. And he still had so much more he wanted to do. On November 2, 1971 – the day before his thirty-seventh birthday – he beat Martinelli, winning re-election by 8,200 votes.

DelBello's win may have delivered only half of the margin he had achieved in his first election, but his hopeful vision and dramatic results had pulled out far more voters. He garnered the largest total vote count of any Yonkers mayoral candidate in history, winning eleven of the city's twelve wards in a fifty percent Republican majority city.

The victory, however, had a disquieting coda. On November 5, 1971, just three days after DelBello's successful re-election, Scher fired the Yonkers police chief, Frank Vescio. The police had opposed DelBello throughout the campaign, likely frustrated by the new collective bargaining process that had displaced their glad-handing approach to get raises out of City Hall. Some were unhappy with a report from the International Association of Chiefs of Police calling for better financial management and organization of the force, noting serious problems with supervision and morale. Scher had asked all staff to remain silent on the report until it could be formally presented to the public. But Vescio went public. Scher was furious. He canned him the next day but backed off the following week, agreeing to make the dismissal a "retirement."

Vescio, eager to retire anyway, withdrew his statement to the press. But the newly elected council wouldn't let it go. Vescio had a twenty-year record as a Yonkers cop and was popular among council members of both parties. That influence would make itself apparent in the coming month.

CHAPTER SEVEN

Days of the Jackals

"We had a deficit?"

DelBello almost laughed. A voter awaiting a morning commuter train into Manhattan had offered the comment during one of DelBello's final campaign stops in the 1971 election. He had been touting the city's rapid progress from a bloated deficit to a balanced budget during his first mayoral term. So quickly had the city's fortunes been restored that some people had forgotten the crushing debt of 1969. "Yes, we had a deficit," he responded. "But not anymore."

In just two short years, DelBello had turned the city around. After a decade of bleeding red ink, Yonkers' budget was back in the black. Millions in wasted local spending evaporated as DelBello reclaimed city control of the incinerator and raised fees for private carters eight-fold. He saved $1.4 million more by eliminating unnecessary positions at City Hall. He even shrugged off an intimidating hail of gunfire through his campaign headquarters window late one night. None of this was magic. It was simply good management, the kind of bullet-proof bravado that Yonkers desperately needed.

There were still urgent challenges. Proper financial management of public services had been neglected for years. The first-term mayor had been negotiating orderly salary increases for public employees. Sanitation workers were on the job without a contract. Many of the city's police officers were unhappy with the new collective bargaining process DelBello had instituted, which had done away with the handshake salary increases of the old days. The state had adopted the Taylor Law to guide collective bargaining among most public employees. Though DelBello supported it, the law had passed before he became mayor. It was his job to implement it. The Policeman's Benevolent Association actively campaigned against DelBello during the '71 campaign, at least partly because of this. The firefighters and civil service employees didn't like it either. Technically, the workers couldn't strike anymore but instead would form unions that would negotiate. Still, work slowdowns and job actions occurred until the unions began to get the hang of negotiations, mainly by bringing in professional negotiators.

That further raised the ire of some city personnel, but not enough to knock DelBello off track. The public knew that padded pockets had been emptied and patronage jobs had been eliminated. Some of the worst political offenders were even facing federal indictments. The citizens who had elected DelBello knew he was changing Yonkers for the better. They witnessed dramatic improvements in their daily lives at a stunning pace they thought impossible merely two years earlier. They saw clean streets, safe neighborhoods and a government that gave a damn about them. In DelBello, they finally had a voice.

DelBello at a re-election campaign event for mayor of Yonkers.

Restless union

But more financial trouble was brewing. Public employees were having a tough time of it as inflation crested like a wave. Teachers, police officers and firefighters wanted the long-overdue contract negotiations to keep up with costs. Westchester County Executive Edwin G. Michaelian had just proposed that one percent of the city's sales tax be diverted to the county. Even the federal government had stepped in to take a piece of Yonkers' pie. Three months earlier, President Richard M. Nixon used executive fiat to push through a ninety-day nationwide salary freeze for all public employees. Their unions' demands for better pay would clash with DelBello's plan for fiscal restraint. Threats of public employee walkouts loomed. The city, having just returned to a balanced budget, would be facing a multimillion-dollar deficit in the coming fiscal year.

With City Manager Seymour Scher's help, DelBello launched the second phase of his planned cost-cutting measures. All of these issues would collide in the first week of DelBello's second term. And the jackals would be waiting for the mayor to get stuck in the mud.

The new year, 1972, loomed even gloomier. Roughly 1,500 municipal teachers walked out on strike due to delayed salary increases and cuts for some employees. The strike went on for ten days and nights, filled with negotiations and setbacks. During the coming week, DelBello and Scher negotiated with the teachers to get them back on the job. The talks worked, and a new contract was signed. The strike ended on January 12.

Just as strike negotiations were concluding, the city's new council convened for its first meeting. On January 11, its first order of business was to issue a resolution requesting that Scher back off on Police Chief Frank Vescio's mandatory retirement. They couldn't override Scher's decision, but this served as a public rebuke. The resolution was approved eight to five. Scher immediately announced his resignation to the shock of his supporters in the audience and even some council members.

With the teachers' strike about to end and a police strike about to begin, the council thought this would be a good time to try to rein in Scher. At least three of the Democrats had been skeptical of DelBello's executive mayoral style. They were irritated that he had hired public managers from outside Yonkers, crippling the beloved patronage they had enjoyed for decades. DelBello noted, with some irony, that many of the city's older politicians "are completely disgusted" with the new honesty in the top levels of city government. "There's no way for the (Democratic) party to get anything out of it," he said on a TV news program. They wanted the city manager as their "guy-Friday," as had been the case for decades. It was a glove-slap. Scher would have none of it.

A resignation averted

DelBello asked Scher not to resign. He said that he hoped "to have him change his mind" on the resignation. But the city manager stood on principle. This was the first chip off the log, he thought. If he didn't resist the council, more swings of the ax would follow. DelBello was distressed. He owed much to the no-nonsense Scher, who had established clear boundaries between his obligations to the mayor's agenda and the demands of the city council. Unlike past city managers, he made it clear that he would do things his own way without council interference. This irked councilmen from both parties. But it got the job done without the patronage and politicking that had plagued previous managers.

DelBello and Scher trusted each other. They both understood their roles. They orbited around one another. DelBello had brought him in, knowing he was an uncompromising professional. What needed to be done in Yonkers was neither partisan nor popular. It was necessary. When confronted by political consternation, even in the quiet corners of their own party, the two had learned to rely on one another. Their professional resolve – and their faithful relationship – were now being tested.

Scher's resignation was not something the council expected. Several council members, including Andrew P. O'Rourke – who would years later succeed DelBello as Westchester County Executive – worried that they had pushed things too far in admonishing Scher's decision to oust Vescio. O'Rourke called Scher, begging him to reconsider his resignation. Even Vescio throttled back his outrage, saying publicly that he always had the highest regard for Scher "as a professional."

DelBello struck back: "The people of this city were just double-crossed by eight councilmen, who a couple of months ago publicly promised support for City Manager Scher and professional government," DelBello told the Yonkers Record. "They picked a time of strife, when the teachers were on strike and other unions (were) making similar charges, to introduce (this) resolution – knowing full well that no city manager with an ounce of integrity would do (anything other) but resign..."

With city manager Sy Scher in Yonkers City Hall for a council meeting.

DelBello immediately called for a special council meeting. He alerted the press in New York City and called countless constituents. A television crew attended. The room was packed. Under glaring lights before the cameras, DelBello demanded that the council take a stance right there as to whether they wanted Scher as city manager. Several councilmen looked stunned and pale.

Local citizen groups showed up in droves to support Scher. The Yonkers Citizens Union, the Lincoln Park Taxpayers Association, the Taxpayers Organization of Northeast Yonkers, the

Yonkers Chamber of Commerce, the Southwest Association of Taxpayers of Yonkers, the League of Women Voters, members of Yonkers' clergy and many other groups called upon the council to reconsider its resolution and take a formal vote expressing its confidence in Scher. They had turned out in record numbers to re-elect DelBello, because of all he had done for the city in just two years – balancing the budget, cutting public waste, driving out corruption and restoring pride in their fair city. They weren't going to stand by silently while the council drove Scher out of Yonkers. There was too much at stake. It was an astounding display of citizen resolve. As DelBello stated later with a smile, "It was a real wing-dinger of a meeting."

The council backed down. It gave Scher a 10-2 vote of confidence. And that was the end of it. Scher, somewhat relieved, rescinded his resignation and returned to work. Del-Bello, very relieved, knew he could continue what he had started. It affirmed what he had always known. Leadership depended on those around the leader – employees, interest groups and especially citizens. He would never take for granted those who voted for him. They showed up when he needed them most.

Knocking on the Capitol's door

DelBello got back to business. The police were the next to threaten a strike. This time the council was more cooperative, working with him to set up a five-person committee to discuss the stalemated police and fire contract negotiations. Job actions began in February and went on for three months, but eventually, a contract was negotiated. Further job actions would take DelBello's time, and he would settle them all. City financing, especially in light of crushing economic pressures, would remain a challenge throughout DelBello's second term. He would again rally his team of mayors and lead the charge in Albany.

Although the Big Six mayors had gotten the state funds they had requested for fiscal year 1972 back in DelBello's first term, new federal shortfalls, fiscal freezes and increasing inflation had taken a bite out of future budgets. The mayors had asked the state to pay all school costs for their cities. The previous deal they had struck would barely hold the line. Having already enlisted Governor Rockefeller's support, they hoped he would join the Big Six in seeking additional federal funds in Washington, D.C. DelBello had recruited support down the chain as well. He had declared February 22, 1971, "Revenue-Sharing Day," urging Yonkers citizens to include written requests for a proposed $10 billion federal tax-sharing bill when filing their taxes. Almost unimaginable today, Del-Bello's polite but persistent manner had a way of spurring quiet but effective action.

Then a wrinkle developed. It looked like the Big Six were going to get shortchanged by the governor. Yonkers' increase in state funding would be close to $700,000 less than planned, a decline in state revenue-sharing from twenty-one percent of state income tax receipts to eighteen percent. Without more funding, local taxes would likely have to increase. The mayors, frustrated with the change, met with the governor again. They told him they had negotiated contracts with their unions based on the twenty-one percent target the legislature had passed. The governor said times had gotten tougher. He told them there was no more money for revenue-sharing.

For the next two years, that would be true. The mayors scrambled to get smaller state bills passed to support specific local safety obligations, including funding for police and firefighters. Those bills had neither the flexibility nor promise of continuance that revenue-sharing would have provided, but they filled the gap for Yonkers. After several months of negotiation, DelBello had secured $4.2 million in additional aid, slightly larger than the original request. Federal aid increased by $13.2 million for urban renewal, police budgets, community action programs and many other projects, bringing the total to more than $20 million. It was a stunning victory.

In October 1972, President Nixon signed a federal revenue-sharing bill that provided money to state and local governments, although far less than New York City or Yonkers wanted. By 1973, the state's economy had improved somewhat. Rockefeller proposed a more generous budget with more revenue-sharing for cities, although there was a general feeling that the state was giving with one hand and taking away with the other – that increased revenue sharing would be offset by Albany's mandate for increased locally funded public services.

Despite the piecemeal, fly-by-wire approach the cities used, they managed to get by, and Yonkers got by very well. The push for increased funding from the state and federal government simply would not have happened if DelBello hadn't once again galvanized the Big Six mayors. His approach was considered an innovation in New York's government. He had an ease with which he reached out to others, inspiring them to join his team. When Democrats couldn't do enough, he reached across the aisle to Republicans. When Yonkers couldn't do enough, he reached out to New York City, Buffalo, Rochester, Syracuse and Albany. When the state legislature and the governor couldn't do enough, he reached out to Washington, D.C. He moved up and down the public chain of command, striking partnerships and recruiting an army of influencers, all in the name of the passionate citizens who had bestowed upon him the honor of public service.

With funding assured, DelBello went on to continue to

solidify Yonkers' success. His popularity arose from his ability to see the city for what it once was and what it could be, rather than resigned-ly managing the sclerosis that had threatened to disable it.

Mayor DelBello marching down Broadway in Yonkers on St. Patrick's Day.

"I ran on the slogan, 'If you want to change Yonkers, a new mayor is a good way to start,'" he said. "People were so fed up with the old way that they voted for me."

He believed in Yonkers, from its gritty Bronx border to its vaulted Hudson estates. There really were no walls between wards. Anyone's problems were everyone's problems. All citizens were connected. And all had to work together to solve their common problems.

A surprise phone call

At the end of 1972, with one year left in his second term, DelBello received a call from Sal J. Prezioso, a lifelong Republican and Rockefeller's first commissioner of Parks and Recreation. He had spent many years changing the face of Westchester, first as County Executive Michaelian's parks and recreation commissioner, and later as his executive officer. He asked DelBello if he could speak with him in person.

The men greeted each other in the mayor's office. Prezioso was direct: He wondered if DelBello would consider running for county executive. The mayor was surprised. He wondered why Prezioso would make this request. He knew he hadn't lost his trust in the four-term Michaelian. DelBello himself believed Michaelian was a good county executive. Could it be a rouse? DelBello remembered back to 1963, when Al Noonan had asked him to run for the Yonkers City Council – only because Noonan thought his buddy Andrew Hayduk could easily defeat an inexperienced challenger and hold on to his post. But this was different. So was Prezioso. DelBello knew Michaelian was tired and that Republican odds for the county seat had been slipping in recent years.

The two parted with a smile and a handshake. DelBello's interest was piqued. He made some phone calls. Everyone had the same opinion: Michaelian would be tough to beat, but it was worth a try. DelBello decided to run. It was a decision he would never regret. Neither would the citizens of Westchester.

CHAPTER EIGHT

(County) Executive Suite

At the beginning of 1973, national anxiety was rising as fast as inflation. President Nixon had been linked to a criminal break-in of the Democratic National Committee at a hotel complex in Washington, D.C., in a scandal that Americans would come to know as "Watergate." While Nixon built his defense, his associates began contemplating an exit strategy. The Vietnam War had bled like an arterial wound into Laos and Cambodia, while the blood of the American economy – gasoline – had practically run dry. Drivers searched daily, vainly, for a few gallons of gas. American exceptionalism had become a casualty of war on both foreign and domestic fronts. It was not a good time to be a politician.

Yet DelBello was putting the finishing touches on what would be his final year as the successful mayor of Yonkers. Through teacher strikes, police and city council rebellions and cuts in state funding, he had turned the city around.

He was proud of the work he had done, but he was hesitant

about a third run. It was a low-paying, politically challenging job. He still had to make a living for his family. DelBello had been thinking about returning to the private sector when Prezioso, a Ph.D. in education and revered statesman of New York's Republican Party, asked him to consider throwing his hat into the county executive ring. He thought DelBello's innovations and tough stances, even against his own Democratic Party, marked him as the kind of independent leader Westchester needed.

At the time, DelBello kept their conversation confidential. He had wondered why Prezioso was encouraging him to run against his old friend, the eminent and capable four-term County Executive Michaelian. Then, rather suddenly, Michaelian dropped out. Later, everyone learned Michaelian had quietly passed the word inside Republican Party circles that he was off the ticket. Seeing what the two-term mayor had done for Yonkers, Prezioso had thought it was time to talk.

The bipartisan candidate

Now DelBello was sitting in an office at Westchester's Democratic headquarters in White Plains. The Republicans were in disarray. For the first time since the creation of the county executive office in 1939, a Democrat could win. William F. Luddy, the former Westchester County Democratic Committee chairman, thought it was the best opportunity for a Democratic county executive candidate he had ever seen. Max Berking, the current chairman, knew DelBello's record of achievement in Westchester's most populous city might earn him the seat.

Berking had run against Michaelian himself in 1969. He lost by 18,000 votes, the smallest margin in any Westchester county executive race. Westchester had a four-to-three Republican voter edge, and Michaelian had been popular during his sixteen-year tenure. But the Grand Old Party's advantage had been steadily shrinking. Michaelian's departure signaled a rare opening in Westchester's top slot.

Luddy and Berking knew DelBello had the ability to attract Republican voters. He was a principled fighter. He had stood up against conventional thinking in his own party. As a Democratic mayor in Republican-leaning Yonkers, he had always worked across the aisle, especially during the tumultuous confidence vote for City Manager Scher. But Yonkers was merely a training ring. The county executive seat was the middleweight battle. The position controlled a 6,200-person bureaucracy with a budget of $245 million. His victory would place him in the national limelight.

DelBello agreed to run, with several conditions – the same stipulations he had demanded in earlier political contests. He wanted a clear field. It would be hard enough for a Democrat to win the seat in the solidly Republican county without a bruising primary. A unified platform would be a striking counterstatement to the Republicans' internecine mud wrestling. DelBello believed some Republicans, dissatisfied with their party's chaos, would cross the aisle to vote for a bipartisan Democrat.

His other condition was the same one he requested of the Yonkers City Council when he became mayor. He wanted to pick the top three positions in each department. Patronage would have no place in his administration. He knew this was the reason for his success. He had always known it. It was his long and abiding belief in professionalism. The two men agreed to both conditions.

Not everyone was on board. The liberal-leaning Democrat William Cowan wanted to distinguish himself. Cowan would compete against both the Democratic and Republican candidates on the small but influential Liberal Party ticket, claiming that his opponents were two sides of the same coin. He would soon find out that wasn't true of DelBello. But it remained a concern for the Democrats, as Berking himself had gotten 8,500 Liberal votes in 1969, thinning Michaelian's margin. He was worried DelBello would lose without the Liberal Party endorsement.

By March 15, DelBello was the party's county executive nominee. His nomination was conferred by acclamation at the convention. Luddy and Berking had kept their words. The Democratic Party was unified. The real fight would begin.

Republicans in disarray

No one in the Republican Party seemed happy with the candidates vying for Michaelian's seat, certainly not Michaelian. Leonard Berman, M.D., Michaelian's executive officer after Prezioso, was considered a smart, competent leader. He had been the Mount Vernon supervisor for a decade before serving at the county office and was the early-on favorite. But he was Michaelian's "no" man who had raised the ire of many Westchester Republicans trying to curry political favors for their districts. By February 1973, he had lost his edge.

The most likely primary victor was Edward Vetrano. He sought to distinguish himself as a party outsider despite his county clerk job in White Plains. His workingman's populism capitalized on a simmering resentment many south-county Republicans had toward White Plains party "elitists." The bulk of his support was concentrated in a crescent of Republican-leaning population centers from Yonkers to Mount Vernon to New Rochelle. But his combative parochialism had a chilling effect on up-county Republicans and other party regulars.

James F.X. O'Rourke, DelBello's old Yonkers mayoral rival,

was in the running as well but dropped out before the convention, siding with Vetrano and securing his own position as the Westchester County Republican Committee chair.

The other contenders included Daniel F. McMahon, the retiring sheriff, who thought his law-and-order image would make him a strong candidate but who had been a Michaelian antagonist. The two men had had several public feuds over funding for the police training academy and the county executive's successful move to place 140 deputy sheriffs under the county's civil service. McMahon challenged Michaelian in court and lost. (This ongoing feud between the sheriff's office and the county police would later drive DelBello to create a unified public safety department under county executive control.)

Michael Roth, a wealthy, young attorney from Rye, was also in the race. Roth had held no prior political office, but he was bright, successful, and adept at promoting that business success. Charles Pound, the sometimes-controversial commissioner of parks, recreation, and conservation, had served Michaelian for twelve years. That likely didn't sit well with the pro-Vetrano rebels. He would soon be struck from the list of contenders.

By the March 12th convention, Vetrano had locked up the Republican Party's endorsement. His ascendancy was anything but unifying. McMahon and Roth vowed to fight on to the primary. Later, Vetrano and McMahon would accuse Roth of excessive campaign spending. Vetrano finally secured the nomination in the June primary, but he was far short of a majority. Only a third of Republicans went to the polls. He took just over forty percent of those votes. McMahon and Roth split the remainder. It was the first county-level Republican primary fight in modern memory, one that caused much stomach-churning among the party leaders.

Michaelian had seen all of this coming. It explained Prezioso's urgent visit to DelBello's office several months before
Michaelian's departure became public. Michaelian's sixteen-
year stability as county executive had made the seat look solid
for Republicans. That complacency was his party's mistake,
and he knew it. Now the sharks were circling.

But Democrats were worried too. DelBello's pass on the
Liberal Party endorsement had pushed candidate Cowen into
the race. DelBello was not concerned. He had stated publicly
that he welcomed Liberal Party support but wasn't going to
spar for its formal endorsement. He knew that playing to the
center in a year with so many disaffected Republicans was the
winning strategy – as it would be for President Joe Biden in
the 2020 presidential race. It was also his belief, refined after
four years of sparring in Yonkers' political ring, that he needed
to remain a bipartisan Democrat. He knew it took people from
both sides to get things done. Progress drove his political
strategy more than the party did.

"I'm accustomed to running just as a Democrat. Staying
on one line gives a candidate more independence. I don't think
I'm losing any votes," The New York Times quoted him as
saying of the Liberal Party's decision not to endorse him. "If
people believe in what we're telling them, they'll find our
name."

Even the way he worded his statement – what "we're"
telling them and finding "our" name – spoke of his message of
unification and teamwork. Not even three full months into the
campaign year, DelBello was already reaching across the aisle.

Managing a countywide campaign while remaining faithful to his job as the mayor of Yonkers was a sleepless task.
Many of the programs he established relied on state and
federal grants. Continued funding for daycare, youth development, jobs, affordable housing, education improvements and
urban revitalization was a huge management challenge.

Reaching out to voters

Reliving his shoe-leather days from his first Yonkers races, DelBello walked Westchester for almost a year, meeting people face-to-face. It was the kind of campaign that had never been done on a countywide scale. To the public, both DelBello and Vetrano were relatively unknown. But one of them showed up at the door.

"I walked every commercial street and shook hands with every merchant in Westchester," DelBello later recalled. "The average person never saw or heard of the county executive, but most of them had heard of the mayor of Yonkers."

Westchester's sidewalks weren't his only stomping ground. DelBello had been beating the streets of Albany and sometimes Washington, D.C. for financial and legislative help for years. It was an inexorable trudge, making up for a decade of urban neglect in Yonkers prior to his mayoral tenure. But prices were rising, the economy was stagnating, and state funding was tight. Many programs, including daycare, had been hurt by state cutbacks. DelBello continued his work with other New York mayors, pushing Albany to take over welfare and education funding. He petitioned state legislators to create a "property tax exclusion," allowing Yonkers to increase property taxes above state limits. This averted the need to increase income taxes, something that would hurt the average voter – a majority of whom were renters – in a budget. Some Yonkers citizens were upset, but most of the city council supported him – including Andrew P. O'Rourke, the most influential Republican council member. They understood that the higher property taxes were needed to maintain a better quality of life and the higher property values that DelBello's administration had generated.

DelBello was sometimes frustrated by how citizens reacted

to public spending. They didn't understand how much the city's success hinged on public funds. They often disregarded debt and decline when it occurred. But they reacted – sometimes viscerally – when their city spent money creating new housing, repairing schools and paying down debt. People sometimes forgot how bad things were before DelBello made them better. He thought back to that citizen's comment on the 1971 campaign trail: "We had a deficit?"

Additionally, many didn't realize how much of the improvement DelBello had made in Yonkers came from government grants and other sources of public funding, not from taxes. Increasing property taxes was needed to complete the investment profile in Yonkers and show state and federal grant sources that the city was committed to its own improvements. Getting that aid directly resulted from DelBello's ability to team with other cities, mobilize state and federal money and create lasting changes in government. He had taken control of the city's finances, created a system of financial audits, centralizing purchasing and boosted its credit rating. All these things required some belt-tightening. But it had been stunningly successful. Yonkers had gone from an urban car wreck to a well-oiled machine in less than four years.

Soon, however, DelBello discovered that other Westchester locales weren't sharing in Yonkers' success. He was shocked by the absence of enforced zoning codes in some Westchester towns. He visited Lake Mohegan, east of Peekskill, where the owner of a beauty parlor described overcrowded neighboring residences, piles of garbage and a failing sewage system that sometimes backed up into her business' basement. Many municipalities had adequate zoning and health enforcement, but many did not. The absence of any countywide standards or enforcement was hurting economic development. If he could do for Westchester what he had done for Yonkers, the county would fare far better economically.

DelBello also discovered that Westchester lagged far behind other counties in receiving state funding. The county was missing out on sizable grants, either because it didn't know about the money or didn't apply for it. He cited millions upon millions in state funds that Nassau County had received for narcotics addiction, community college, youth programs and libraries. Westchester had received little or none. As DelBello observed, "Yonkers alone will spend $400,000 enforcing its building and environmental codes. Half of this amount would be reimbursed by the state if Westchester County adopted part of the state local-option law."

His positions during the campaign were innovative and forward-looking. He wanted to bring more affordable housing into Westchester. He wanted a Westchester rent freeze rather than the Rockefeller-endorsed rent stabilization program advocated by his opponent. He demanded a mediation process so that landlords and tenants could negotiate reasonable rents and ensure better quality housing. He wanted more extensive public transportation. He sought a reduction in crime rates. He believed that welfare could be restructured with the aim of achieving full employment. These were the type of things DelBello had successfully brought to Yonkers. Now he would bring them to Westchester.

DelBello traveled to Albany with the Westchester Tenants' Alliance to urge Rockefeller to impose a temporary rent freeze. This gained him populist points as an independent fighter. He was the Democratic pugilist in the Republican ring, fighting for the citizens of Westchester against the opposing party's fiscal failure. He relished his insurgency. Vetrano couldn't step out of the Republican line, especially after alienating many in his party. He could only watch in anguish as DelBello fought for the people.

An 'October surprise'

When fall rolled around, DelBello participated in a series of debates against Vetrano and Cowan. Vetrano's message was to keep doing what had been done under Michaelian. He criticized the corruption, financial mismanagement and poor planning in Yonkers – all of which was true before DelBello became mayor.

DelBello punched back. He had decisively ended Yonkers' graft and patronage. He erased the $12 million debt – entirely the doing of Vetrano's own party – in his first two-year term. He detailed how he had fixed Yonkers by calling upon other mayors, the governor, the state legislature and congressmen for assistance. He had brought tens of millions of dollars in state and federal grants into the city for urban renewal, youth programs, education, the arts and the environment. His administration made Yonkers one of the greatest urban success stories in the entire state.

He wished, however, that Westchester's muscle had been available to him. Imagine what could be done for Westchester's cities and towns if the county played a bigger role in galvanizing local power? DelBello went on to propose a countywide office of consumer affairs, women's work programs, youth development initiatives, daycare and access to state and federal funding for housing and jobs. He saw the urgent need for solid waste disposal, public transportation, regional hospital care, and drug treatment. He believed the county could team with its municipalities to help them access upstream government grants, attract businesses and reduce taxes. Help cities and towns help themselves, he said, with the county as an incubator for civic improvement and public wealth. It was as good a business model as it was a political one.

DelBello's visionary proposals were a stark contrast to Vetrano's clipped, black-and-white responses. He never took Vetrano's bait. He criticized his "coattail candidacy." He knew the same professional government strategy that had worked in Yonkers would work for Westchester. "Why stay the course?" he challenged Vetrano. DelBello had used the debate stage to make the election a mandate between stagnation and change. Viewers and listeners were transfixed. Even Republican voters watching the debates were embarrassed to see the legendary accomplishments of a young, energetic, idea-driven mayor panned as a failure by a tenured county clerk.

The election's "October surprise" came right on schedule. Republican Assemblyman and former U.S. Attorney J. Edward Meyer from Chappaqua endorsed DelBello. Meyer had already worked with him on a state rent control bill and was impressed with his "open government" and "regional approach" to problems such as mass transit and drug addiction. The endorsement wasn't entirely unexpected. Meyer wanted Westchester to deal with the looming problems of solid waste disposal, public transportation and crime. He liked Michaelian and thought he had done a good job during a period of relative economic stability. But after more than a decade-and-a-half, he believed the county needed new ideas and stronger management to help cities and towns chart an increasingly uncertain future. DelBello, he said, "will best set a tone of moral leadership."

The New York Times' endorsement came a week before the election: "Mayor DelBello has been an active, enlightened municipal leader who has earned esteem for stemming the spreading blight in Yonkers, revitalizing community areas, providing residents with improved public service while eliminating a budget deficit and holding down local taxes." The "Gray Lady" knew he would do the same for Westchester County. Noting that many other county Republicans had already endorsed DelBello, The Times called Vetrano's record "followship" rather than leadership. It urged voters to elect DelBello.

The Gannett Westchester-Rockland Newspapers – the owner of a group of municipality-identified newspapers, including The Herald Statesman in Yonkers which is today known as The Journal News – refused to endorse anyone, criticizing all three candidates, including the rarely mentioned Cowan. Gannett took particular umbrage with Vetrano, noting that his bitter primary feud had targeted Leonard Berman, whom the paper felt would have been the ideal Republican candidate. While Gannett attributed DelBello's success in Yonkers solely to City Manager Scher and predicted he would be "hamstrung" as county executive, the paper nevertheless referred to him as "charismatic" and "a proven vote-getter." It was a backhanded compliment that he could live with. DelBello regarded the indecision from the Republican-leaning news company as a de facto endorsement of his campaign.

'It looks like you're going to win'

As soon as polls began to close on Election Night, excitement rippled through DelBello's campaign staff. His poll workers were monitoring some solid Republican districts where he had expected to lose decisively. The early numbers showed Vetrano was barely squeaking by. Although he wasn't doing as well as expected in his hometown of Yonkers, more encouraging numbers rolled in. David Barshovsky, a pollster on loan from Representative Ogden Reid's campaign, called DelBello at Yonkers' Carvel Inn (now the Royal Regency Hotel) and urged him to head to the Roger Smith Hotel in White Plains, where his election-night campaign party would be held.

Before DelBello could ask the big question, Barshovsky added with carefully harnessed delight, "It looks like you're going to win by a small margin." Forty-five minutes later, DelBello arrived at the hotel. He walked into the small ballroom where Democratic regulars were gathering. The room exploded in applause and cheers. Luddy and Berking came up and shook his hand enthusiastically. The dream that had started at an election office conference table ten months earlier was coming true.

Indeed, DelBello hadn't done as well in Yonkers as he hoped, largely due to a weak Democratic candidate in the mayor's race against Angelo Martinelli. But he still won his hometown by 1,000 votes.

Elsewhere, DelBello was running well ahead of his rival. Vetrano's intra-party civil war had taken a toll on the Republican establishment. His south-county rebellion fizzled. In the process, it alienated solidly conservative north-county strongholds. New Rochelle, the tip of Vetrano's Republican crescent, fell to DelBello. Even the Republican fortresses of New Castle, Yorktown and Pound Ridge voted for DelBello by a small margin. He even edged out Vetrano in his hometown of Greenburgh. By the end of Election Night, DelBello had won by 2,728 votes countywide, a mere one percent of voters, and a number that would grow to 3,366 during the recount. But in solidly Republican Westchester, it was a Democratic knockout.

Cowan hadn't had much of an effect in stealing votes at all. It was later discovered that he had only spent $639 on his entire campaign. Perhaps after a couple of months of watching DelBello, he secretly wanted him to win as well.

Vetrano doomed himself. He tried to be an in-party rebel and a conformist at the same time. A politician running on an incumbent platform always has the party's weight behind him – and around his neck. In his fight for the nomination, Vetrano had tried to be two different candidates at once. Had he remained the dutiful Republican soldier and unifier, he might have won.

But even if Vetrano had kept both gloves in front of him, he was in the ring with DelBello. That may have been a challenge too great for any Republican to bear. Yonkers was his proving ground; Westchester politics, his next audacious fight. Republicans nationwide were struggling with hyperinflation, wage freezes, Watergate and Vietnam. Citizens were battered, exhausted, and scared. DelBello was Westchester's great new hope.

This was his biggest political fight to date, but it wouldn't be his last. Many challenges lay ahead. The Republicans would recuperate from this round and come back for more. DelBello would fight two rematches in the county ring before entering the heavyweight competition of the lieutenant governor's race. Always the optimist and exquisitely well-trained, he would be prepared.

CHAPTER NINE

The Rainmaker

Outgoing County Executive Ed Michaelian had known all along that DelBello was the best choice for his replacement. Michaelian was considered "Mr. Republican" in Westchester. But he had been shoved aside in an ugly Republican internecine war in which his own administration was characterized as a group of "White Plains elites" who didn't care about the down-county working man. That was untrue. He was deeply concerned about the county's future.

Michaelian liked DelBello. He thought he was a visionary and had done a great job in Yonkers. Even a small dustup between him and City Manager Sy Scher when DelBello was mayor of Yonkers was conveyed in the local news with a cheeky flare, like two friendly opponents at the same cocktail hour. Michaelian felt far more antipathy toward his own party for having marginalized him during the county executive campaign.

Shortly after the 1973 election, he and his wife Joyce

invited DelBello and his wife Dee to dinner at their home. Michaelian gave DelBello some inside information about the county – weaknesses in his own administration, things he thought needed to be changed. He had, after all, supported many things DelBello thought were important – a new regional medical center, a merged county police force and regional management of the county's trash. He met with DelBello after the election to give him a snapshot of the county's finances. Michaelian was leaving DelBello with an $8 million surplus from the previous year's budget. It would be applied to reduce county taxes in 1974. The new budget was also expected to produce a $1 million surplus by the end of the year. But, as DelBello knew, the days of surplus were about to end. He would need to save every public dollar to avoid raising taxes – one of his key campaign promises.

DelBello was also well-aware of many of the problem areas, his own beloved Yonkers being a crucible of sort for the county's socioeconomic challenges. But there were many places he hadn't explored, including some of the north-county towns with their quaint, small business districts and rural lands. Those lands were under threat from rapid growth. Real estate investments might be on hold as the worst of the recession washed over Westchester, but the growth was inexorable.

Meeting the new county executive

One place Michaelian had wanted DelBello to see even before he took office was Muscoot Farm, a magnificent 777-acre preserve of active farmland in Katonah acquired by the county in 1967. He hoped DelBello would continue his legacy of preserving these vital vestiges of open space as the county grew. Michaelian arranged for the DelBellos to tour West-chester on a sunny November day. Muscoot was one of their first stops. It was here that DelBello would create one of his greatest environmental legacies.

Years later, Dee recounted Michaelian's kindness and the pressing need to preserve Muscoot Farm. "Ed Michaelian was very polite to both of us after the election. I think he was relieved that Al had won. He knew the Republican candidate was not a strong or competent leader. He showed his kindness by loaning us his white county Cadillac and telling us to take a ride in it around the county to inspect all the facilities and parks. It was on that day that we discovered Muscoot. Al told me that the plans were to raze the historic farm mansion and outbuildings and construct an ice-skating rink. We were horrified and vowed that that would not happen."

Michaelian also introduced DelBello to 400 of the county's chief businesspeople at the Westchester County Association's annual membership dinner. Standing together before a packed room at the now-defunct Rye Town Hilton in Rye Brook, the two men received a standing ovation, perhaps as much a tribute to their bipartisanship as an expression of hope in troubling times. Many of the association's members were Republicans, accustomed to decades of their own party's political leadership in Westchester. DelBello understood how important business was to the future of the county. He assured them of his support. But he also asked for their support in return for public initiatives that would require their collective financial commitment – investments in public transit, social programs, consumer protection and wastewater treatment. None of these things would be easy to accomplish, but they would all be vital to the county's economic health. He convinced them that their own financial success was entwined with the well-being of the county as a whole. He wasn't asking merely for their support of spending initiatives. He wanted their involvement as leaders as well.

Michaelian personally introduced DelBello to the board of legislators, a newly formed body that had recently replaced the more populous, unruly board of supervisors. The new seventeen-member legislature was predominantly Republican, as all things had been in Westchester. DelBello knew, as he had during his time in Yonkers, that bipartisanship was the only way to get things done. He also knew many of the legislative members fairly well through his years in politics, particularly a newly elected Republican representative – his old adversary and occasional ally on the Yonkers City Council, Andy O'Rourke.

Across the waters of Long Island Sound, former Nassau County Executive Eugene Nickerson was thrilled to see a fellow Democrat take Westchester's reins. Nickerson had been a groundbreaker in county politics, having been elected as Nassau's first Democratic county executive since 1912. He served from 1962 to 1970, when he was succeeded by Republican Ralph Caso. An icebreaker and an innovator, he established programs that his county had never seen. He wanted DelBello to know what he had done and how he had done it. DelBello was thrilled to have Nickerson's help.

He tapped the Long Islander to be the master of ceremonies at his inauguration, which took place in the new Westchester County Courthouse, a building that would soon be found to be plagued with construction and design problems. The ceremony was celebratory, featuring local office holders, clergy, business leaders, labor representatives, young people, senior citizens and entertainment personalities. Michaelian was there, as was Ogden Reid, the Republican-turned-Democrat congressman who had been so helpful throughout DelBello's campaign. Max Berking, the chairman of the Westchester County Democratic Committee, introduced the judge who would administer the oath of office.

At that moment in history, the Watergate investigation was underway. The economy was in a recession. The country was frightened. DelBello's speech, though frank, was optimistic. Before a crowd of 500 people, he implored citizens: "Help me to overcome the crisis of confidence in our public officials. As for my part, I pledge this administration to be more open and responsive to the people, knowing that we can live up to our high ideal and make government work for all of us."

Setting up shop

With wages stagnant, investments crippled, fuel-driven inflation squeezing the wallets of citizens and purse strings of government alike and homebuilding down thirty-seven percent from a year earlier – a record drop for the county – it was an unenviable time for anyone to take office.

DelBello knew he needed to assemble the best staff he could to battle the economic hydra. He picked J. Robert Dolan to be his "executive officer" – today, deputy county executive, the number-two post in county government. (The job title was a holdover from Michaelian, who was familiar with the term, having served as a naval officer in World War II.) Dolan had been the Mount Kisco village manager for five years before becoming assistant city manager in Yonkers. DelBello believed Dolan had both the professional qualifications and the right "up-county, down-county perspective" to be able to perform well as executive officer.

He also had the right Democrat-Republican perspective. Dolan's first charge was to review existing top county management. There would be no "head rolling" of prior Republican appointees. Changes would be made as warranted. This was a brilliant strategy, especially for the first-ever Democratic county executive. Unlike the corruption he had faced in Yonkers, DelBello recognized that the Republicans had run a stable and professional county for sixteen years. "We don't intend to clean house," he said. "It's hard enough finding good people without removing good people."

Among those he kept on board was planning commissioner Peter Quintus Eschweiler, who would help DelBello develop housing plans and open space initiatives. He also kept Genevieve Leary, Michaelian's transportation commissioner, who would help him put together an ambitious public transit plan. Other Republicans who remained in their posts included County Health Commissioner Jack Goldman, M.D., Public Works Commissioner Robert Dennison and Environmental Facilities Commissioner William Borghard.

Dennison was soon succeeded by Frank C. Bohlander, a Republican, who served on the Board of Acquisitions and Contracts, which voted on all contracts awarded by the county. Keeping a Republican in place was brave, daring, and consonant with DelBello's bipartisan sensibilities.

Some Michaelian appointees were slated to leave, but DelBello permitted a number of those to stay on until their retirement dates so as not to jeopardize their pensions – an act of decency and principle. Said one anonymous department head: "He is very professional. He didn't have to be that nice. He understood us and treated us like professionals. I think that the county has a winner." Many of the Republican employees DelBello kept on staff soon became his greatest friends and strongest political advocates.

The move was a pleasant surprise for many elected Republicans, including the board of legislators with whom DelBello would work for the next nine years. It would serve him well. His decision not to "clean house" meant that he was far more interested in getting things done than playing

DelBello with wife Dee visiting their friend and Mayor of Jerusalem Teddy Kollek. DelBello's strong push for bipartisanship emulated Kollek's dedication to improving Israeli-Arab relations.

politics. But he had to seek approval for all his appointments from the Republican-dominated board. His bipartisan approach made the board far more accommodating. He didn't want to banish the Republican Party. He simply wanted to make his administration work.

DelBello brought in his first senior black policy leader, Orial Redd, to coordinate the administration's human development programs. Having previously served as program director for the Urban League of Westchester County Inc.,

Redd had the broad perspective and expertise needed to coordinate the county's human service resources. She initiated programs to help senior citizens, youth and the economically disadvantaged. She also advised DelBello on state and federal human service grants.

New math

Each appointee for an agency leadership position in DelBello's administration needed a two-thirds majority from the board of legislators. Most of the appointees he designated got the nod by a substantial margin. One of them, however, was a close call – his nominee for commissioner of parks, recreation and conservation, Joseph Halper. Because Halper lived outside the county, his nomination required a two-thirds majority. The final vote was 11-6 in favor. All six Democrats on the board, as well as five of the eleven remaining Republican members, voted to confirm. Republican Board Chairman Thomas F. Keane Jr. ruled that the required majority had been reached. In DelBello's view, it hadn't. He ended up fighting against the vote to approve his own appointee. But why?

He and the other Democrats knew this was a setup. If eleven votes were considered a two-thirds majority, the Republicans – conveniently, eleven in all – could override any veto DelBello enacted on a legislative measure he didn't like. Keane argued that two-thirds of seventeen is 11.3, so rounding down to the nearest whole number was acceptable. DelBello argued that fractions aren't full votes. So, what was a two-thirds majority – eleven votes or twelve?

Democrat Vincent Rippa said the "favorable" vote on Halper was intended to set a precedent for defining a two-thirds majority. The Republican majority had waited for a required two-thirds vote on a matter – any matter – to test-run its definition of a majority.

"It was staged," Rippa said. "If they get away with eleven votes being a two-thirds majority, they will be able to block everything DelBello does."

The board of legislators hadn't had to deal with this question before. Years of Republican dominance in the executive and legislative branch made the two-thirds majority a moot issue. County Attorney Harry Lott – soon to be replaced by DelBello's appointee, Gerald Harris – believed twelve votes were required for a two-thirds majority. It was a fortunate decision from a Republican holdover. Keane, arguing legislative preeminence, strongly disagreed. DelBello then was in the unusual position of petitioning the New York State Supreme Court to get the favorable decision for his own appointee invalidated.

It worked. Supreme Court Justice John Marbach ruled unflinchingly that twelve votes constituted a two-thirds majority. That meant any such majority would require at least one Democrat voting with the Republicans, at least in this legislative session. DelBello and Harris, who had become county attorney by the time of the decision, were pleased. DelBello planned to resubmit Halper's nomination, but after Keane made it clear that it was going nowhere, Halper himself withdrew. It was a pyrrhic victory, complete with a sacrificial lamb, but one that would protect DelBello against future veto overrides and partisan splits.

Running on empty

The first real crisis of the young DelBello Administration was the gas shortage that resulted from the 1973–74 embargo by the Organization of Petroleum Exporting Countries (OPEC) in response to U.S. support for Israel and the Yom Kippur War. Lines of waiting cars snaked a quarter-mile down major thoroughfares, snarling traffic and flaring tempers. DelBello created dispensation rules that limited fill-ups to every other day, in accordance with the last number on a license plate – odd or even. A more obscure anti-hoarding rule said that only those with a half-tank or less could fill up. That meant station staff would check their customers' fuel gages before pumping. But the reaction of some customers to this intrusion was rather tactile; one such intrusion resulted in a woman hitting a gas station attendant in the head with her purse, bringing new meaning, in service station parlance, to the term "battery."

It was the first mandatory gas restriction program in the state of New York. Governor (Charles) Malcolm Wilson – who succeeded Nelson A. Rockefeller when he resigned in December 1973 to head the Commission on Critical Choices for Americans – had made such procedures voluntary. But in the more densely developed automobile enclave of Westchester County, something had to be done quickly. At least one-fifth of the county's gas stations, according to Internal Revenue Service (IRS) agents, were selling fuel above the already-pricey legal ceiling. Fights were breaking out in gas lines when people tried to cut in front of one another.

In his first two weeks on his new job, DelBello established a citizens committee on energy conservation to study the gas shortage and make recommendations for immediate action. It resulted in several options, the most sensible of which was the rationing plan. DelBello took his idea straight to the public. Unhappy gas station owners crowded a White Plains hearing room, claiming that the move would alienate their "regular" customers who, in an age of more parochial commerce, were the bread-and-butter of their businesses. Concerned that out-of-town fuel-hunters would crowd out the regulars, they condemned the proposed restrictions. DelBello listened, letting them vent their frustration. But he knew the regulations were needed. His brand-new Office of Consumer Affairs was alarmed by a widespread refusal of stations to sell to non-local drivers. Halfway through February, his second month in office, DelBello proposed a county law mandating odd- and even-day gas sales linked to license plate numbers. The law was quickly endorsed by the board of legislators in a bipartisan 13-2 vote.

Despite the initial objection from station owners, the sixty-day emergency legislation immediately calmed consumer panic. Knowing that more limited daily sales wouldn't run stations dry, gas lines became more orderly. People, though still annoyed, had confidence that they could get their half a tank. Station owners saw an end to the chaos. In less than two months, DelBello had succeeded in taming one of the most frantic crises the county had ever faced.

Yet he knew fuel rationing wasn't the end of it. The tight gasoline supply was in part due to the Federal Energy Office limiting shipments to New York. But it was the state that allocated gas to counties. DelBello began pushing the State Emergency Fuel Office in Albany to supply more gas to Westchester. He convinced the agency that he was doing more than his part by making mandatory Wilson's voluntary program of alternating-day gasoline sales. That was a selling point. Albany, understanding that Westchester was already out in front on this, began shipping more gasoline to the county. "We can now hope for enough gasoline to cover the needs of our residents," DelBello said. By the middle of June 1974, the county had been relieved of its worst gas crunch, and Westchester stations were seeing steady increases in supply.

In his first six months in office, DelBello had taken some of the most far-reaching steps of any county executive in New

York history, making Westchester a model for the state – and the country – in managing the gas crisis. It was the first of many pressing issues he would take head on and win. Once again, as had been the case when he became mayor of Yonkers, he had difficult financial challenges ahead of him. This time, however, they were not the result of mismanagement, but rather national financial trauma. Unemployment was at a post-Depression high of seven percent, and the country was plagued by an energy crisis and rapidly rising interest rates. Managing Westchester would be a tough job.

As the economy worsened, state and federal funding would be instrumental in advancing DelBello's agenda. His skills as a financial rainmaker in securing government funding was one of his greatest strengths. His selling point was in explaining to state and federal agencies why the money mattered. He was able to convince lawmakers, the governor and eventually the president of the United States, that county government was the inflection point for a strong economy and better quality of life and that it warranted their attention.

Financial ringmaster

By July, gas supplies had stabilized, but daunting financial challenges were on the horizon. Although Michaelian had left him with a generous surplus, DelBello could read the tea leaves. He had kept ten percent of the county's 6,700 jobs vacant. He fully expected $7 million in unanticipated spending, largely because of rising fuel costs, depressed tax revenues, inflation and public assistance for all the additional citizens who had lost their jobs. DelBello was vigilant about keeping county taxes from rising. But continued inflation, high unemployment and depressed consumer spending meant citizens' needs were going up while tax revenues were going down.

He appointed Vincent A. Matrone as the commissioner of finance. Matrone was a top-notch accountant and no-nonsense fiscal hawk from a prestigious accounting firm in New Jersey. Some Democratic Party regulars were annoyed by DelBello's out-of-region picks, but Luddy and Berking had accepted that non-negotiable condition when they asked DelBello to run. Matrone established an "encumbrance system" that removed all expected future expenditures from the budget and placed them in an interest-bearing account. When the bill was paid months later, the interest would be returned to the general fund. It replaced the county's antiquated cash-disbursement system with strategic investments. In a period of runaway inflation, this kind of fiscal juggling was revolutionary, especially for government. The protocol earned the county hundreds of thousands of dollars in interest. It also earned DelBello's administration the respect of the business community.

He put it plainly: "We are talking about standard money management procedures seldom used in government. We have to get a $1.10 in services for every dollar of taxpayer money." He noted that private companies do this all the time. Why shouldn't government do it?

Assistant commissioner for finance David Shulman, who later assumed the top financial post, praised DelBello's ingenuity. He noted that DelBello had a knack for thinking outside of the government box. He believed that his capabilities in finance, paired with his professional, nonpartisan management style, saved Westchester millions. "Al was the ultimate politician without being political," Schulman said.

Those business skills were invaluable and rather rare for a politician. Westchester was weighed down by several enormous financial obligations that had preceded DelBello's time in the executive's seat. The federal government had mandated closure of the Croton Point Landfill. The only workable solution was for the county to incinerate its trash. It was an expensive undertaking. Every government in the nation was doing everything possible to cut energy costs. He thought, "What if the county built an incinerator that generated power at the same time?" The trash had to be burned anyway. Using it as fuel to drive a turbine and make electricity would turn a financial burden into low-cost energy for the county. DelBello had read about a still-experimental technology that turned garbage into energy. It had the potential to cut high electricity costs and eliminate the county's trash problem for pennies on the dollar. It would take a monumental, multiyear investment, but DelBello would eventually solve both problems at once, saving the county tens of millions of dollars.

Trash was but one of many pressing matters, including the need for regional hospital care, public transit, improved highways, job and welfare assistance and housing. All required investment exactly when investment opportunities were expensive and scarce. DelBello turned to the state. With Democratic Governor Hugh Carey at the state's helm since the beginning of 1974, DelBello petitioned the assembly to appropriate $50 million in financing for a solid waste disposal program, new sewer plants in several mid-county towns, new facilities at Westchester Community College and reconstruction of the Cross County Parkway in Yonkers.

He paired fiscal austerity with ambitious county programs, drawing on both county and state financing to prime the pump. His efforts paid off. By March 1975, a little more than one year into office, Moody's Investment Service gave Westchester County its highest credit rating. This was exactly the opportunity DelBello had hoped for. At that time, Westchester Medical Center, the county's long-planned health care endeavor, was nearing completion. The center had been financed with $61 million in state-authorized loan obligations at a relatively unfavorable rate. Because of the county's credit upgrade, DelBello was able to issue county bonds immediately and short-term notes at much lower interest rates than the state loans. The move saved the county $40 million in interest costs over the thirty-year life of the bonds. Without missing a beat, he immediately redirected those savings toward financing the county's $60 million share of the planned waste-to-energy plant. Together, these pivotal projects and several others would transform Westchester into one of the wealthiest and most successful counties in the nation.

DelBello, the visionary, the synthesizer, the master juggler in the center ring of the nation's financial circus, was able to keep all the balls in the air, balance budgets while proposing massively ambitious new projects, trade red ink for black and do what anyone would have thought impossible even in a good economy. He had a fearlessness to deliver what he had promised. But this fearlessness wasn't reckless. It was his unflappable belief that government could do so much more than it had in the past. During one of the worst economies since the Great Depression, DelBello was building Westchester into one of the greatest financial successes in the county's history – and the country, for that matter.

Birth of the Bee-Line

Arguably the most important campaign promise DelBello made was improving the county's faltering public transportation system. It functioned adequately on major routes but was insufficient for the county's increasing population and commercial destinations, particularly during a recession and gas shortage, when people relied on it more than in the past. With bus companies under increasing financial stress, proposals to cut routes and reduce frequency were being proposed.

The sixteen bus companies in Westchester were privately owned. Each had a proprietary interest in its own routes, ostensibly a positive motivation in a healthy economy. But this amalgam of discrete, private decision-making resulted in poor coordination. It got much worse when the economy tanked. Bus routes that connected to one another operated with little regard for the timing of pickups and drop-offs. Tickets for connecting buses had to be purchased separately. Bus shelters were in disrepair or absent altogether. Rider information about routes and times was difficult to find. These things discouraged ridership, which drove down revenues even further during a period of increasing costs.

DelBello hoped to double the number of buses in Westchester and increase the number of routes. Roughly 85,000 people – about ten percent of the county's population – depended on buses. Some used buses as their primary means of transit, others to connect with trains headed to and from New York City. Even DelBello's assistant commissioner of finance, David Shulman, had taken the bus to the train station for years prior to accepting his county job. Now the viability of the transit system was being stressed by high fuel costs and a sagging economy. By early 1974, the companies were losing close to $1 million per year. Routes were being cut, and bus frequency was reduced, making life even more difficult for those who depended on street transit.

Nassau's Republican County Executive Ralph Caso had recently taken over the bus transit system in his own county, making it a public entity. It would be a disastrous economic decision. DelBello understood the benefit of keeping the system in private hands. But he wanted the bus fleet to operate seamlessly, as if it were a single, coordinated system. He wanted the county to work with the companies to coordinate, plan, and advertise their services better. And he wanted citizens who needed buses to be served properly. He believed assisting them with a capital infusion from the county would provide services where they were needed. A more reliable, predictable and better-coordinated system would attract more riders, thus reversing the companies' decline. It was the birth of Westchester's first public-private enterprise, and it would be a winner.

DelBello understood the financial difficulties bus companies faced. As mayor of Yonkers, he had single handedly ended a brief bus strike. In an unusual move, he had gone to Bronxville's Lawrence Hospital (now New York-Presbyterian Lawrence Hospital), where the president of Club Transportation, Peter Gallagher, was a patient. DelBello and a mediator worked with Gallagher to resolve the strike. That late-night move showed a level of commitment and trust that no one had seen from a mayor before. It earned DelBello the trust of the bus company.

DelBello's reputation for earnestness would help him greatly in his county executive role. He met with the company leaders and garnered agreement to create a regional bus service. It was a good deal for everyone: The bus companies would partner with the county to develop a seamless regional transportation plan, one with the appearance of county control under the "Bee-Line" moniker. The county would purchase new buses and lease them to the bus companies at favorable rates. The companies would handle operation and maintenance. They agreed to hold fares at 35 cents, increase connections, reinstate recently canceled routes and provide transfer tickets for all connections, regardless of which company was operating which route.

Part of the companies' financial difficulties was a consequence of state law that restricted street transit entities from operating lucrative charter services. Years of private lobbying had kept them out of the charter game. Private-only charter services and school-bus companies raked in cash while transit companies suffered. DelBello had what he thought was an acceptable idea – allow transit companies to operate charters at off-peak times to cross-subsidize their expenses. It would generate extra revenue without denting the charter industry. But that decision required a change in state legislation.

By March 1974, DelBello had filed applications for more than $13 million in state and federal aid to improve bus transportation. The money would be used to purchase ninety-five new buses and build 100 bus-stop shelters. He also filed a package of laws that would give the county broad control over bus and taxi operations and provide bus companies relief from sales, excise and fuel taxes, while allowing them to conduct off-hour charter operations. A month later, he convinced the Board of Legislators to endorse a proposed state transit bill by a remarkable 15-1 vote. No county in the state had ever sought the public transportation authority Westchester was seeking. It was now April. DelBello had been in office for three months. Westchester was on the verge of revolutionizing public transportation in the state of New York.

By May 1974, the bill was dead. Angelo Martinelli, Del-Bello's 1971 mayoral opponent and now mayor of Yonkers himself, had surreptitiously conveyed a letter of protest to State Senator John Caemmerer that kept the bill in committee. Martinelli had never commented to the board of legislators or made any other objection known. He stated he was concerned that possible route changes could hurt Yonkers. His arguments were parochial and meritless. In the following months, public transportation services in Yonkers would decline rapidly as costs increased.

Nassau County's Caso was also opposed to the bill, stating that he felt it would jeopardize the growing regional public transportation system he had joined. It was, however, the mounting costs of that poorly considered decision that threatened him. Westchester's transit connections to New York City remained unchanged, controlled in large part by the Harlem, Hudson, and New Haven lines, owned and operated by the city's Metropolitan Transit Authority. Buses connecting to Westchester train stations might even boost MTA revenues. And connections to Nassau County were minimal. So why the objection? Caso had hoped that if Westchester joined the regional public network, its tax contribution would help defray his county's hemorrhaging costs. Nassau was running onto the financial rocks and wanted Westchester to help bail it out.

Despite the financial pressures, the Westchester County plan was providing better service and giving the companies some financial relief. Although the state legislation failed, additional state and federal transit grants were rolling in. In early 1975, DelBello created the county's Department of Transportation and charged it with developing a unified countywide bus system by coordinating routes operated by sixteen private bus companies and establishing a uniform fare structure. Consolidated bus schedules appeared in all transit locations, newspapers, and county brochures. All vehicles bore the county's new logo – the "triple banana," as it was euphemistically called, forming a modern-looking "W." The buses were painted in the same color scheme, and all operations were coordinated through the county's Department of Transportation. The public was barely aware that their countywide bus system was being operated by sixteen privately owned companies. It was a first for New York State.

Westchester developed an amended legislative package that would open the bus companies to charter service while avoiding competition with existing private charter companies. In 1975, DelBello returned with a much better and well-considered bill. The state legislature shot it down again. The state was still squeamish about conferring its transit licensing and regulatory control to Westchester. Eventually, enabling legislation would pass that gave DelBello some of the things he needed to make the county's transit system work.

But he wasn't waiting for the legislature to act. He continued to secure state and federal funding to improve services and keep the fares stable. He introduced the new "Uni-Ticket," which combined Westchester's bus service with the MTA's rail service, using one ticket at more reasonable prices. DelBello, who served as the leader of the Urban Affairs Committee for the National Association of Counties (NACo), met with President Gerald Ford the following year to pitch his ideas for this flowering public-private partnership. The Republican president, who had succeeded Nixon when he resigned amid the Watergate scandal, liked his innovative ideas, proffering more federal funding for Westchester transit.

In this, DelBello was assisted by Genevieve Leary, his transportation commissioner and a holdover from Michaelian's administration. She was professional, knowledgeable and remarkable in that she was a woman working in what had traditionally been a male-dominated profession. She had some philosophical differences with DelBello over the extent of county involvement in transportation management, but she never quibbled with him publicly. After several years, Leary made the decision that the two would be better off if she departed.

Though disappointed, DelBello brought in a new transportation commissioner, R. Raleigh D'Adamo, to replace her. A former MTA executive, D'Adamo was highly qualified. Yet he needed help with the more nuanced transportation management approach to Westchester's diverse, suburban structure. So, he decided to bring on board a newly minted consultant to help him navigate his job – Leary herself. DelBello smiled when D'Adamo informed him of his hire. Both men knew her knowledge of transportation was encyclopedic. It was an ideal role for her. Never one to micromanage his staff, DelBello had given D'Adamo the green light to run the transportation department as he saw fit. It was the unique mark of his leadership and an inspiration to those who worked for him.

D'Adamo went on to create a comprehensive five-year bus plan, using a panel of experts from outside the transportation field. A number of them were the business leaders DelBello had met through Ed Michaelian during the transition. They knew public transportation was essential to their ability to attract the best employees. They had implored county leaders to "run buses like a business." With DelBello in the "driver's" seat, that would finally happen.

During the next several years, Westchester's transit system made tremendous gains. The county built 150 new bus shelters – at no cost. DelBello arranged for the construction contractor to recover all the expenses for building the shelters from advertising displays on the shelter walls. These shelters, so vitally important to the success of the bus transit system, were put in place using only market incentives.

The county later invested more than $8 million in much-delayed federal assistance for the delivery of 105 new "kneeling" buses, with wheelchair lifts to make boarding easier for those with mobility challenges. Westchester quickly earned awards, including a citation from the state department of transportation, for having the most cost-effective system in New York. By 1977, DelBello had delivered on his promise of increasing public transportation throughout the county. Buses were on time, with many more service runs than in the bleak days of 1973. Routes were expanded. Ridership increased dramatically. Transit companies were earning a profit under Westchester's "triple banana" banner. And governments throughout the nation were making a "Bee-line" to Westchester to see what other interesting ideas this innovative county executive had up his sleeve.

Flying high

Bus transit wasn't the only political football in Westchester. The county's growing business eminence was increasing pressure to make the Westchester County Airport a business hub. No longer did executives from Larchmont and Armonk desire to drive more than an hour to John F. Kennedy and LaGuardia International Airports in Queens when flights could be boarded minutes away from the office.

But the airport was under-equipped. The World War II auxiliary fighter base was outdated. Terminal facilities and even runways needed to be expanded to accommodate the growing demand. The airport, once situated among the apple orchards and spacious estates of Rye Town, Harrison and New Castle, was now home to burgeoning suburbs and corporate headquarters. Increasing corporate air traffic and suburban growth were on a collision course.

The airport had been privately operated for nearly three decades, but the operator's lease was approaching its 1977 expiration date. DelBello and Public Works Commissioner Robert Dennison knew that a county-run airport would provide an important financial bonus. Roughly $400,000 in additional revenue annually was at stake, ten times more than the county received under the paltry private lease that was about to end. It would also give the county more latitude in planning the airport's use and expansion and in dealing with noise and safety concerns.

But it would give the county more headaches as well. Complaints about noise had long been the lament of Rye Brook and Greenwich residents. They were concerned about safety as well, after several crashes had occurred that, fortunately, affected no one on the ground. The county applied for and received a license from the federal government to install an "instrument landing system," or ILS. Despite the safety benefits, some worried that it would increase air traffic that would otherwise be shunted to other airports during inclement weather.

In August 1974, Greenwich filed a lawsuit naming the county and the Federal Aviation Administration as defendants. Greenwich was particularly irked about noise from private jets – which were not subject to government noise control standards as were airlines – and nighttime landings. Rye Town parachuted into the melee, claiming the proposed ILS system would actually increase crash risks during low-visibility landings, despite data to the contrary. Anthony "Chappie" Posillipo, Rye Town Supervisor, was opposed to the ILS for that very reason. He threatened that Rye Town would take legal action if the ILS were approved.

Ultimately, Greenwich dropped its lawsuit, and Rye Town backed off in return for certain concessions. DelBello and Deputy County Attorney Sam Yasgur were able to hammer out a "parliamentary" solution that created a legal agreement between Greenwich and the Westchester board of legislators, among others. The agreement was guided by a Joint Airport Committee composed of residents, officials and pilots to identify problems on an ongoing basis.

After two years of squabbling between DelBello and the board of legislators, they finally reached an agreement in which (the now-defunct) Pan American Airlines would manage the airport through a five-year renewable lease. The board of legislators passed resolutions abandoning construction plans for an additional runway and imposing a flight curfew from ten p.m. to seven a.m. DelBello's plans for the future of the Westchester County Airport were finally getting off the ground.

Consumer protection balancing act

Another of DelBello's sweeping campaign promises was to create a county consumer protection agency. At the time, a small consumer protection division existed in the Office of the Sealer of Weights and Measures. It didn't do much, and its location seemed curious to many. That particular department happened to be in the sheriff's office. Long considered to be a "policing" issue – one that would ostensibly crack down on consumer fraud – the office's location might have seemed sensible to some.

The Office of the Sealer of Weights and Measures was a division of the state government. Although the sealer, Kenneth Hale, and his staff of ten didn't report to the sheriff, the office's location created barriers for citizens, especially blacks who, more often than affluent whites, were the victims of consumer transgressions. Contacting and visiting an office in Valhalla full of white sheriff's deputies was more than an inconvenience. For many black citizens, it was intimidating.

Though the sealer's employees weren't police, they were still considered "peace officers." They checked the accuracy of scales and measuring devices at food markets, gas station pumps and energy meters and ensured the safety and labeling of food. This was an important part of consumer protection, but certainly not all of it.

The idea of consumer protection had become politically popular, especially with the advent of more regional shopping, new services and the ascent of consumer watchdog Ralph Nader on the national scene. The consumer protection functions in the sealer's office were inadequate for the economy of the 1970s, especially during a time of economic stress and limited family resources. Creating a new and upgraded office as a department of the county executive seemed like a sensible idea.

Ed Michaelian had also been in favor of a consumer protection agency and had programmed $100,000 for a small division separate from the sheriff's office. But he ran into resistance from his own Republican brethren on the Board of Legislators. DelBello correctly believed a consumer affairs agency in the county suite would provide political responsiveness and be supported by other county agencies, especially finance and social services. That was something that couldn't be replicated by the office of the sealer.

DelBello was already strengthening consumer protection within his own administration. In his first month in office, he established a volunteer division of consumer services under his control. By March, it had handled 225 complaints and obtained $9,946 in refunds for frustrated consumers. During that same period, the sealer's office – with a larger staff – dealt with seventy complaints and got consumers $2,100 in refunds. Clearly, the demand for consumer protection was far greater than what the county had previously provided, and the sealer's office was doing far too little.

Yet the Board of Legislators, knowing that consumer protection was one of DelBello's key campaign promises, had tried to scuttle his plans before he took office. At its final meeting of 1973, the board suddenly proposed an expanded consumer function under the sealer. The public reaction was furious. At the new board's first meeting in January, citizens angrily complained of unfair trade practices and political obfuscation. They considered the board's proposal a violation of the separation of powers in the county charter. Why should the county's legislature be able to appoint this one department in a state bureaucracy, and why should that department remain in the sheriff's office rather than in the county office building?

Many shared DelBello's position that county executive control of consumer affairs would make the office much more accessible, allow input from other county agencies and encourage additional volunteer staff. Its visibility would help access state and federal funds to expand operations without dipping further into county coffers.

Republican legislators tried to argue that the location of a consumer complaint office was simply a matter of government efficiency. But it was a preemptive power play, pushed by the newly elected Republican sheriff, Thomas Delaney, the first salvo in a series of confrontations with DelBello, who would ultimately seek to combine the independent sheriff's office with the Parkway Police.

District Attorney Carl Vergari stepped into the fray, supporting DelBello's position that consumer affairs was a county executive function. Being a Republican himself, he offered a compromise that the Board of Legislators might accept. He suggested a "Consumer Protection Board" made up of the district attorney (himself), County Attorney Gerry Harris, the county executive and the chairman of the Board of Legislators – a bipartisan split. One additional person, likely a Republican, was later added to his proposal. The office would have up to ten people staffing it who would be able to investigate consumer problems and report back to the Consumer Protection Board. Any urgent legal matters could be forwarded to the county attorney or the district attorney. It seemed like a good compromise.

It wasn't. Despite overwhelming public testimony favoring the DelBello plan, the board seemed destined to keep the consumer office with the Sealer of Weights and Measures. DelBello decided to request an opinion from the state's legal office. In a surprising twist, state Attorney General Louis Lefkowitz ruled that the Sealer of Weights and Measures should be under no department in county government but answerable only to the state sealer's bureau. It was for DelBello a half-victory, but better than no victory at all. DelBello could not give the sealer additional powers, though he could more effectively supplement Ken Hale's work with his own legal staff and volunteers. As had always been the case, using his own resources to support the work of other non-county departments would win him the admiration and loyalty of the sealer's staff.

DelBello's revised proposal established a Division of Consumer Affairs located within the county's executive office, but oversight would come from a bipartisan board. His staff would support the sealer's work. The department would focus on civil rather than criminal remedies, with hearings and a conciliation process. The law would mandate timely delivery of products and an implied warranty requiring a refund within thirty days if goods were found to be defective. Charges for home or car repairs could not exceed 120 percent of the written estimate. Part of the new proposal included development of a code that would stipulate everything from repair service obligations to licensing of repair staff and contractors.

Yet as late as 1975, the proposed bill and consumer code had languished. In mid-summer, Edward Willing of Mount Vernon, a stalwart conservative opposed to countywide consumer legislation, dropped a revised bill in front of the Board of Legislators that did away with a new office and staff. DelBello and the Democratic legislators were outraged. The new draft dumped the responsibility for enforcing the new county code right back in the state sealer's office. Audrey Hochberg, a Democratic legislator from Scarsdale, said the sealer's office would be overwhelmed. DelBello accused the board of wasting the county's time and the taxpayers' money. He called the maneuver "a blatant breach of agreement" that raised serious doubts about the board's competence. He felt like he was back in Yonkers, fighting petty turf wars with the city council.

Further public hearings on the amended proposals repeated

the angry hearings of early 1974. People felt the Republicans on the board were doing a political end-run around their financial security. The legislature coughed up a slightly toned-down version of Willing's bill. The proposed legislation blatantly violated Attorney General Lefkowitz's separation-of-powers mandate. One Democratic legislator said she couldn't support it. DelBello pledged to seek state enabling legislation that would allow county executive authority for the position.

By summer's end, the board voted in favor of the two bills. DelBello was happy to sign the bill creating a consumer code. The legislation created new and important protections for consumers. A second bill creating a new county agency separate from the county executive's office was adopted. DelBello vetoed it, knowing the Board of Legislators would override it. They did.

While disappointed in only getting half a loaf, DelBello was not overly concerned. The new code gave the sealer some real teeth, including subpoena power and the authority to conduct public hearings. The consumer affairs controversy had given the Democrats some real political red meat, likely resulting in the 9-8 narrowing of the board's Republican majority just two months later. DelBello would push for more funding and staff in the next budget cycle. But he had already done the most important work. The consumer affairs office was taking hundreds of calls per month and returning tens of thousands of dollars to frustrated consumers. It was reshaping the way businesses operated in Westchester. And it was reinforcing the idea that government led by a principled, visionary professional could improve the lives of citizens.

CHAPTER 10

Mr. 'Why Not?'

The word "antagonist" derives from the Greeks, meaning "opponent, competitor, rival." In theatrical circles, the antagonist is the character who opposes the protagonist, the story's hero. In politics, it is largely the same. Though the conflict is burdensome, the protagonist's successes are ultimately defined by the resistance of the antagonist; even the antagonist might be transformed through a subtle reciprocity and rapprochement. Neither all good nor all bad, both characters are shaped by context. Each needs the other to achieve their aspirations. And sometimes – in rare moments – they form an unspoken alliance, a muted empathy that helps them both. Adversaries in life, friends in posterity, each is ultimately grateful for the challenges from the other that helped them stake out their own place in the world.

Enter Angelo Martinelli

In DelBello's story, Angelo Martinelli looms as an early antagonist – one who, having lost his first Yonkers mayoral race
to DelBello in 1971, finally staked out his territory as DelBello's
successor, opposing the county executive at every turn. It was
ironic: The man who had once been Mayor DelBello would
have reveled in a county government trying to help his
hometown. Not so, Martinelli.

In his most recent move, he had refused to sign an agreement with Westchester to create a county Criminal Justice
Coordinating Council (CJCC). The council, mandated by the
state and accompanied by ample funding, would have leveraged important federal grants to help fight crime and better
manage the criminal justice system. But the CJCC was a
tripartite agreement between the state, the county, and all of
Westchester's municipalities. Martinelli argued Yonkers should
get a bigger share of the funds. If Yonkers didn't sign it,
everyone could lose the money.

It was one of many ongoing disagreements. Shortly after
Martinelli had become Yonkers' mayor, he began undoing
many of the programs DelBello had begun. He stopped the
Urban Renewal program in its tracks, concerned that out-of-
town minorities would flood the new apartment buildings. He
canceled the program to rebuild Getty Square, eliminating the
overpass that would have linked two portions of the area. The
only I.M. Pei structure that remained was a parking garage.

All of this was compounded by Martinelli's efforts to scuttle bus-related state legislation, his resistance to a countywide
solid waste disposal plan, and his insistence on having his own
manpower program to deal with unemployment. All DelBello
could do was sigh. He didn't dislike Martinelli, but he wondered why he continued to run against him rather than his

opponent in the upcoming mayoral election. It was like a reenactment of 1971.

By December 1974, however, the relationship turned around. Perhaps it was the cost of upgrading the city's solid waste incinerator, which was sending Yonkers' budget into the red. Perhaps it was just battle fatigue. In any event, Martinelli decided to bury the hatchet. He had good reason to do so. Speaking in the city council chamber just before a preliminary budget hearing, he commended DelBello for offering a county budget with no tax increases. That was important to him. He felt DelBello was putting his concern for Yonkers ahead of politics. He suggested a joint city-county task force to review both governments' programs and look for both savings and better coordination. Everyone breathed a sigh of relief. DelBello was immediately gracious in the press. Taking Martinelli's cue and running with it, he applauded the mayor for a "good, constructive statement." He said he would contact him the next day, noting that the county could be of some help in relieving Yonkers of its fiscal burdens. In the coming years, though the relationship between the two men would not be without controversy, they began to work together on many issues important to both Yonkers and the county. For DelBello, this wasn't about trying to make amends or carrying a torch for his hometown. He was simply doing his job for everyone in Westchester – including Martinelli.

The two would team up to tackle one of the biggest crises of the mid-1970s – skyrocketing rents. Earlier, Martinelli had canceled urban renewal projects that DelBello had started, only to discover that the curtailed supply was colliding with rising management costs in existing units – and with the law, resulting in a suit from the federal government regarding housing discrimination. Now he was on board with DelBello and many urban leaders to get a bill through the state legislature that would restrict rental increases.

Martinelli, along with the mayors of the other Big Six cities – the organization that DelBello first established when he was mayor of Yonkers – went to Albany to plead their case for state rent legislation. DelBello joined other county executives in meeting with state Senate Majority Leader Warren Anderson. They were opposed to a ten-cent-per-gallon gas tax, even though the receipts would be shared with the counties. Every move the legislature made seemed to rob Peter to pay Paul. The counties needed real relief.

The state had enacted the Emergency Tenant Protection Act in 1973, a law to limit rent increases. Though well-intended, the county's Rent Guidelines Board, created under the law, was considering fourteen percent increases for one-year leases and 19.5 percent increases for three-year leases. It was far too much for most tenants, now deeply stressed by the recession. A state court judge issued an injunction to halt the high rates.

By 1975, DelBello requested that Governor Hugh Carey step into the fray. DelBello was sharply critical of the Rent Guidelines Boards, largely because they had no clear direction or parameters. They were ineffective. "The best proof of that," he said, "is that rent guideline boards in Westchester, Nassau and New York are all in court." The issue bounced around in the courts for several years, with landlords often winning their cases. But without the legislation and the fight organized by Westchester's majority-tenant population, it was likely that citizens would have fared far worse. On this issue, DelBello and Martinelli were on the same side.

That same year, DelBello sent a message to the board of legislators asking for passage of a county bill authorizing returning tax funding to Yonkers that had been lost when the county began to collect a one percent sales tax from munici-palities. This had occurred prior to DelBello's term as county executive. Michaelian needed the funds to meet county budget demands. At the gala celebrating the end of DelBello's mayoral tenure, he had been asked tongue-in-cheek by Councilman Dominick Iannacone if he could get that money back to Yonkers when he officially became county executive. He smiled and said he would try. Once again, he delivered by excluding Yonkers from a countywide sales tax increase affecting other cities and towns. At least for the moment, his sometimes-antagonist Martinelli was quietly, deeply grateful.

Championing women

The early 1970s had marked a sea-change in the rising influence of women. Both in the workplace and society, women were actively fighting for equality against a long, powerful tide of suppression, one that had begun to crumble when women finally won the right to vote a half-century earlier. DelBello supported this effort, but as the new county executive, he had to make his position quite clear. He got that opportunity right away.

Late in 1974, Sheriff Thomas Delaney, another antagonist, abruptly and falsely announced that DelBello had cut the newly created rape investigation squad from the sheriff's 1975 budget. Women's groups were livid. Most were not aware that DelBello didn't control the sheriff's budget. The squad remained intact, and public ire quickly shifted to the sheriff.

Indeed, few leaders in Westchester had done more to elevate the status of women in government and the private workplace than DelBello. In August 1975, there was a large rally at the Westchester County Office Building in White Plains to celebrate the fifty-fifth anniversary of the 19th Amendment to the U.S. Constitution, giving women the right to vote. Legislators, organizers and local leaders attended. DelBello addressed the crowd, stating his firm belief in the Equal Rights Amendment.

"The sad thing of today's society is that it takes legislation and not just goodwill and simple good sense to obtain equal rights for women," he said. Subsequently, the first countywide women's conference took place at the Westchester County Center. A record 4,000 people showed up for a series of speeches and ongoing workshops. Clearly, the impetus for greater involvement of women in business and politics was thriving in Westchester. DelBello was more than fully on board. He was part of the movement, and his top picks for his administration reflected it.

He established the Task Force for Women in 1975. The office became a clearinghouse for greater female employment, addressing discrimination in the workplace and increasing women's presence in government – including the county executive's office. It was the first such county program in New York State, serving as a model for three other counties and two cities. In 1980, it became the Westchester County Office for Women, a centralized, permanent, community-based resource to address the needs of women and families.

DelBello hired some of the most prominent working women and political experts in the region. Beside Orial Redd – the first black to work for him in county government, as an assistant – there were senior assistant county attorney Cheryl Bradley, Judith Glazer of the Office of Community Services and Katherine Hayden in the Department of Social Services. He didn't just "go with the program." His administration was the program.

Working it

From the start of his administration, DelBello had wanted to work closely with labor. But the recession of the mid-1970s made this imperative. With large numbers of laborers laid off, the economy had sacked worker contribution accounts, especially in the construction field. The Laborers International Union of North America (LIUNA) was facing financial collapse. Retirement and health benefits were at risk.

Keith Drake helped DelBello to secure money from the federal Comprehensive Employment and Training Act (CETA) program. The funding was designed specifically to help local and regional governments support work projects for laid-off laborers and retrain workers with new skills, without displacing existing government workers. DelBello wanted to use the money to hire unemployed labor, mostly construction workers, to undertake backlogged county construction projects. The county hires would only earn fifty to sixty percent of the prevailing wage and were limited to a total of $10,000 in salary. In return, the county would cover the full costs of their benefits, relieving LIUNA from a financial crash. It was small but decent pay, and it would get workers back on the job. There was some grumbling at first, but the unions and their workers agreed.

Hundreds went back to work in a program reminiscent of the Depression-era Works Progress Administration. Laborers began repairing fountains at the Kensico Dam, painting the county office building and building an addition to the museum at the Ward Pound Ridge Reservation, among many other things. It was daring, unprecedented, and it meant that workers kept their homes and unions stayed afloat. Taxpayers benefitted through public projects completed at a lower cost than would have been possible during a good economy. It was simply one of the most innovative things any government had done. In a time of great fear and financial uncertainty, DelBello had stitched together the public and private sectors into a seamless enterprise – one for all and all for one. Everyone made compromises so that no one would go broke. In the end, the unions respected DelBello, even the Republican-leaning AFL-CIO. They would never forget his support.

Construction wasn't the only sector in economic trouble. Tarrytown's General Motors plant laid off 2,000 workers, largely because of fuel shortages and high interest rates. It was, according to DelBello, "The worst blow to employment in the county in my memory." Westchester took a bullet in the other knee when the gargantuan Anaconda mining conglomerate closed its offices in adjacent Greenwich, Connecticut, laying off hundreds of additional Westchester workers. All in all, Westchester saw a 100% rise in unemployment in one year.

Westchester's workforce development office became the lynchpin of job and skills retraining in the region. From the very beginning of his administration, DelBello worked with Drake to form the Westchester Labor Advisory Council to address job losses and better position the county for federal grants. He had always believed in the importance of labor professions in public life and had planned to strengthen the power of labor and their unions, regardless of the economic pressures the county faced. By 1975, the county had acquired $1.3 million in federal funds, distributed among the municipalities, to boost the number of workers for a host of local government purposes. Drake initiated an economic development program focusing on promoting small businesses – still the most important job generator in the county and more predictable than large multinational companies. All these job training and economic development programs kept unemployment down to 5.3 percent – close to three percentage points lower than the national average.

It was easy to overlook these accomplishments. After all, Westchester was still in the midst of a painful recession. But it was so much less painful than it would have been without DelBello's leadership. The metaphorical tables, where worried families reviewed their budgets and squeezed their pennies, were in the kitchens of the homes they still owned and rented. Westchester was surviving. What many people didn't know was that, by national comparison, Westchester was thriving.

The doctor is in

As the county worked toward the grand opening of the Westchester Medical Center, small community health facilities were still the only go-to option for many low-income Westchester residents. This kind of primary care was often avoided by people without the financial resources to see a doctor about an emerging condition, often resulting in more serious conditions that required more expensive hospitalization. Perhaps no one appreciated DelBello's work in advancing health care more than Rev. Jeannette J. Phillips. A Peekskill resident, Phillips had spent most of her life advocating for nonprofit community health centers. A member of Westchester's Black Democratic Party caucus, she was alarmed by the paucity of health care in Westchester's poorer urban communities. She and a group of other black women began meeting at Peekskill's United Methodist Church in 1971 to push for a health care facility that would serve economically disadvantaged people within their community.

She got DelBello's attention. Working with his newly appointed health commissioner, Jack Goldman, M.D., and assistant commissioner, Phyllis Koteen, M.D., Phillips established the first community health-care clinic using county funds. By 1975, she had acquired a grant to open the health clinic. Yet she had difficulty getting the right executive director to keep the clinic going and needed more substantial funds to attract the right staff.

Phillips called upon DelBello for assistance. He provided her with in-kind staff until she could get the clinic on its feet. Ann Coughlin had been working in the county health department under Koteen. She was transferred to the position of interim executive director of the clinic. Having an experienced county health professional leading the health center got it up and running. The start-up was successful. After its reopening in 1977, this single Peekskill clinic exploded into the Sun River Health system, with forty-three clinics serving 245,000 people today.

Phillips praised him, not only for his profound concern for the well-being of citizens but also for his extraordinarily egalitarian ethic as a political leader in the 1970s. She was always comfortable engaging him.

"As a black woman, I always felt comfortable in Al's presence," she said. "His was a real warmth, not just politeness. He truly listened."

Triumphs and setbacks

For the remainder of DelBello's first term, he initiated programs that would forever change the course of the county, despite a crippling national recession. He started a simple senior discount program in his first year – something taken for granted today. After issuing county I.D.s to seniors, he worked with department stores and supermarkets to generate senior citizen discounts. The program included discount senior bus tokens at half the standard fare, boosting both ridership and local commerce.

"The Senior Citizen Discount Program is one of the accomplishments of this administration of which I am most proud," DelBello said. "I can promise you that we will extend the program to ensure that senior citizens can continue to travel at low cost and move freely throughout our county."

These people, often unable to drive for health or economic reasons, needed transit more than others. Reducing bus fares resulted in more mobility for seniors, more spending capacity, and greater income for the business owners they patronized. The discount program was later extended to the handicapped and, as the recession dragged on, to those receiving welfare payments. DelBello understood the interdependency of an economy – that increasing the average citizen's purchasing power enriched everyone. He also believed that a society must be as compassionate and humanitarian as it is economically productive. If you want society to succeed, everyone has to ride the same bus.

County Executive DelBello inaugurating the Westchester Senior Citizen Discount Card.

DelBello would go on to establish the county's first centralized 911 call center, a new service that at the time was vigorously opposed by the fragmented police and fire departments throughout the county's forty-four disparate municipalities. Sheriff Delaney argued that a centralized system would cause confusion and delays in response time. The ire and defensiveness of police throughout the county was palpable, as difficult as that may be to imagine today. Police forces saw the move as a turf battle. DelBello saw it as a means to save lives.

There were problems with the system at that time, however. The technology hadn't caught up with the concept in 1975, but by the early 1980s, a basic form of 911 was already working in parts of Westchester and Greenwich. The new system could fill in for the lack of coordination between telephone exchanges and jurisdictional lines, ensuring that emergency calls were directed to the right police departments. Still, there was resistance from fire departments and even rural residents who shunned the near-ubiquitous concept of street numbers. It wasn't until the mid-1990s – after the bungled police response to the 1989 murder of Betty Jeanne Solomon by husband Paul's lover, Scarsdale schoolteacher Carolyn Warmus – that a countywide system was finally in-stalled.

DelBello also started the Office for the Disabled, which undertook the arduous task of transitioning people with mental disabilities back into community homes – a vitally important mission at a time when the Willowbrook State School scandal on Staten Island was blaring on the evening news. And he staffed the office with a disabled director and staff. The office advised the county on compliance with federal legislation. But DelBello had established the office in 1975, long before federal regulations were in place to drive local handicapped accessibility in public buildings.

DelBello had committed himself to an office for the disabled during his first county executive campaign and made his new office the first in New York. At that time, as DelBello learned after meeting with a group of disabled people, public policy discouraged disabled employment by removing their social security health benefits if they got a job. DelBello changed that policy so that the employed people with disabilities could keep their health benefits. What bothered him the most, however, was that none of the county offices were handicapped-accessible.

"Everything had to be changed," he said. "The bus system, cutting down curbs, creating access for wheelchairs into the county office building, handicapped bathrooms: Everything had to be changed to accommodate the disabled. It was a very interesting experience," he said. He commented that these concerns led him to think about handicapped access in many other locations, including public transit – leading to Westchester's acquisition of "kneeling buses."

Within his first two years, DelBello's progress as county executive had begun to turn heads. He was selected by Time Magazine as one of 200 emerging national leaders. He was selected by the National Association of Counties to head the association's urban affairs committee. By 1976, he was officially named by Democratic presidential candidate Jimmy Carter to be a liaison between local government officials in New York and the campaign, having been the first elected official in New York to endorse the soon-to-be president.

However, DelBello was not successful at everything he tried. He often lamented his failures quite openly, something almost unheard of in politics. In some respects, it probably helped him by making him the disarming, open book that people came to trust. DelBello had wanted to expand the narrow, four-lane Hutchinson River Parkway into three lanes in each direction. The improvements would essentially be an extension of Interstate 684 from Interstate 287 near White

Plains to the Bronx County line. The original parkway was narrow, winding and outdated for modern high-speed traffic. It was also quite beautiful. Constructed in the 1920s and '30s, the parkway shared rustic characteristics such as stone-arch bridges, wooden lampposts and gently sloped curves along preserved parkland that protected local water supplies.

DelBello's six-lane plan made sense for solving the notorious safety and congestion problems of the antiquated parkway. Designs even included replication of the historic stone bridges that would span a new right of way, essentially creating a second historic parkway parallel to the first that would carry traffic in the opposite direction.

Scarsdale was having none of it. Local citizens quickly formed opposition groups. During contentious meetings in the summer of 1982, community leaders along the route of the parkway opposed the six-lane expansion, arguing that the widening would bring increased traffic, noise and pollution.

DelBello was convinced he could talk his way through the opposition, as he had done with the gas station owners in 1974 and with so many other angry citizens. DelBello's finance commissioner, David Shulman, told him not to attend the meeting with the residents. He said it would be a front-page bloodbath. It was. Ultimately, the expansion was limited only to the area around the I-287 and I-684 interchange and the connection to the Cross County Parkway in Mount Vernon. DelBello was perhaps too willing to engage citizens' concerns head-on. He almost always succeeded in addressing opponents directly. But not this time.

The management of Playland Amusement Park was another shortcoming for DelBello, although a problem that he could have solved had he stayed in office beyond three terms. The beautiful, iconic Art Deco park, perched on the edge of Long Island Sound in Rye, opened in 1928. But by 1969, it was operating at a $300,000 annual loss. In 1980, the county signed a contract with the Marriott Corp. to manage the park and improve its facilities. Two years later, Playland had a $3 million annual deficit. Marriott bowed out. The county was left to hire another contractor and develop a master plan that would ensure the amusements park's rides and concessions would remain in place. DelBello left the county executive's office at the end of that year. The park would eventually be restored under Andy O'Rourke's administration and would be designated a national landmark in 1987.

Despite these setbacks, DelBello succeeded at almost everything he did and made the path easier for those who followed him. He had an innate, deeply anchored understanding of the role of government in restoring and preserving the public's trust. In his first year as county executive, Iona College invited him to present a lecture on the changing Westchester community.

"To be effective today, government must emulate the techniques of management, which are characteristic of successful business organizations. At the same time, government must provide what no business can offer – acute sensitivity and responsiveness to the public – because government, no matter how businesslike, does not run on a profit motive but on public trust accountability."

His words were particularly notable in light of the difficult economy. He led Westchester by thinking outside of the conventional box, by instilling in those around him the belief that Westchester could accomplish anything and by never hesitating to work across party lines. He was motivated by good ideas, by trying things that had never been tried, thereby making the impossible possible. As one of his associates would observe, "Al was always thinking of things. He was 'Mr. Why Not?' He was the political version of 'If you see something, say something.' He was really in it more for the people than the politics."

CHAPTER 11

Trash to Cash

It was an unpleasant bit of news, but not an unexpected one.

For several decades, the Croton Point Landfill had been Westchester's dumping ground for household garbage and commercial waste. Perched precariously on a peninsula jutting into the Hudson corridor, the dump was a disfiguring scar on the cliff-crested façade that adorned the river's edge. Wetlands and small streams had been filled to create more disposal space. Metal drums of undetermined industrial origin had been carelessly punctured over the years. The mounded landfill, sixty feet high and a half-mile across, bled forty million gallons of toxins into the river each year. In May 1972, the U.S. Attorney's office, propelled by the Clean Water Act, filed a federal civil suit against the county.

At the same time, the recently established Environmental Protection Agency warned those cities with active incinerators that their equipment was badly out of compliance with the Clean Air Act. Municipalities had to make substantial capital investments in facility upgrades or shut them down. Croton's charge for refuse tripled to $7.50 per ton – still nowhere near the actual cost of operating the facility. As if in a trash compactor, Westchester found itself being squeezed.

Historically, trash collection and treatment were controlled by municipalities. Incinerators had been built by Westchester's larger cities and towns, including Yonkers, New Rochelle, and White Plains. In those densely populated areas, incineration was the best method for getting rid of the refuse. The leftover ash was trucked to Croton Point. So were all the things that couldn't be burned – metal, glass, broken appliances and all the burnable garbage that exceeded the capacity of the incinerators. For towns that didn't burn their garbage – most of the municipalities in the county – everything went to Croton.

More trash talk

As early as the 1950s, county officials were concerned that the Croton landfill was running out of space. As an interim solution, the Westchester Park Commission planned for the dump to phase out solid waste and accept only incinerated material. The county presumed that Westchester's communities would eventually build more incinerators, cutting the volume of unburned material. The opposite happened. Some plants closed, and Croton's rancid mountain grew.

The problem overwhelmed County Executive Michaelian, making the garbage crisis one of DelBello's first and most pressing issues after taking the oath of office in 1973. Out-of-state options, such as shipping waste to New Jersey, had been considered, but that strategy could never accommodate the majority of the 900,000 tons of trash per year that Westchester generated. DelBello refused to dump his problems upstate.

With Croton on life support, he knew he needed an innovative in-county solution.

Towns could build brand new high-temperature incinerators that would meet federal air quality standards and turn trash into ash – a much smaller disposal challenge. But those plants were expensive to build and operate. But what if those furnaces could generate energy at the same time? DelBello was familiar with "waste-to-energy" technology that used trash as fuel to create power. Steam-generation systems would heat buildings and spin electricity-producing turbines. For years, the county had thrown away its garbage. That was the real "waste." Why not turn that trash into cash? With fuel prices climbing and foreign supplies holding America hostage, making energy from garbage seemed ideal. The new county executive decided to tackle both problems at once.

Waste to energy

Energy costs in Westchester were the highest in the nation, topping $44 per 100 kilowatt hours when other areas were paying as little as $18. EPA rules forced northeast utilities to rely on expensive low-sulfur fuel oil when many other less dense and less polluted areas of the country could burn coal. But that wasn't the only reason for the high prices. Consolidated Edison (Con Ed), the major utility for New York City and almost all of Westchester, charged much more than other utilities, such as the public Power Authority of the State of New York (PASNY), which supplied hydroelectric power to upstate communities at one-eighth of Con Edison's rates.

This was more than a consumer issue. A county report on energy noted that conversations with manufacturers inevitably turned on electricity costs as a major deterrent to operating in Westchester. The report noted that the county had lost approximately one-third of its manufacturing production employment in the previous six years.

DelBello lamented that "Companies that should be locating here don't come near us anymore, and some companies have moved out to the West or Southwest." He added, "The General Motors plant in Tarrytown spends $400,000 a month on electricity, the highest cost of power of any G.M. plant in the world. Whenever there's a downturn in the industry, they close Tarrytown fast, and that means 3,000 blue-collar workers are unemployed."

During the next several years, DelBello would power up a movement for a referendum allowing Westchester to form its own public utility, an idea Con Ed would fight tooth and nail. In the interim, creating energy from the county's trash problem would become an effective end-run around the utility's monopoly over Westchester citizens, and one of DelBello's signature achievements.

The waste-to-energy idea was a great economic opportunity for Westchester, but not the only one. In the days before recycling was widely practiced, valuable materials such as metal and glass had been treated like refuse, adding to the expensive landfill shortage the county now faced. Though much of the material couldn't be burned, it could be recovered, reused and resold. Glass and metal from the waste stream would be sorted, recycled and marketed for secondary use. Even the ash left over from incineration could be mixed with asphalt to pave roads. For DelBello, it was an entrepreneur's dream, transforming a pricey problem into a perpetual economic resource.

The technology worked. But it wasn't cheap, it was still new, and it certainly wouldn't be feasible in the local arena. This project required a countywide plan. DelBello had to get all of Westchester's cities and towns on board. That would be a bigger challenge.

Working through New York State's Environmental Facilities Corp., a public benefit entity and an arm of the Department of Environmental Conservation, the county developed its first solid-waste management plan. By early 1974, the initial plan was complete. It recommended a highly coordinated waste management system administered and financed by the county to serve all of the county's municipalities. Different elements of the trash management process – collection, shipping, recycling, incineration – would be orchestrated among different locations, but all towns would be part of the same system.

Certain locations would extract glass and metal from the trash. Other locations would shred garbage to make combustion more efficient. Trucks would cart material between local "transfer stations," recycling centers, incinerators and a new landfill for any unburned or unprocessed material that remained. No other county in the United States had coordinated waste management on this scale. The expected efficiencies were revolutionary. Westchester's municipalities would save a fortune.

The county planned to take over four incinerators – New Rochelle, White Plains and Yonkers and one of the five other remaining plants. They would be upgraded as required by federal law. A new "thermal conversion" unit – the waste-to-energy incinerator – would be constructed on the 600-acre county-owned Grasslands site in Valhalla. The facility, located on the site of the future home of the Westchester Medical Center, would provide heating, cooling, and electricity for the hospital, medical school, penitentiary, and other facilities at the Grasslands. DelBello believed using county land for a major construction project would prevent the perils of public resistance. He would soon find out he was wrong.

The cost of the plan was significant – $105 million dollars. It was a big tab, but it would be financed over thirty years. And there would be state matching funds. The New York State

Department of Environmental Conservation (DEC), pressed by the federal lawsuit to help solve the county's disposal crisis, established a grant program to cover forty percent or more of the project's expense, significantly lowering the county's bond obligations.

It wasn't a free ride for municipalities. "Tipping fees" – the per-ton amount a town pays to dump garbage – would increase. A charge of $15 per ton, double Croton Point's fee, would be needed to cover the operation of the facility and repayment of the county's bonds. These fees would also finance local incinerators, establish new transfer stations and pay for county trash vehicles – costs that the municipalities currently bore. Given the services the county would provide and the high cost of other alternatives, this was a good deal.

The plan would relieve several cities – Mount Vernon and Yonkers in particular – from the gargantuan cost of building or upgrading their existing incinerators to meet EPA standards. The higher disposal costs would also encourage local recycling to reduce the tonnage of refuse hauled to local transfer stations. DelBello circulated the plan to local officials. Most, regardless of party affiliation, welcomed the idea.

Yonkers and Mount Vernon chase pipe dreams

But not everyone was on board. Yonkers' Mayor Angelo Martinelli and certain members of the city council resisted. Yonkers immolated its trash in one of the incinerators DelBello wanted for the county system. But the city's garbage-burning plant had been long fraught with mechanical failures, corruption and incompetent management. In 1969, just before DelBello became Yonkers' mayor, the twenty-year-old incinerator was plagued with repeated breakdowns and contract mismanagement. A new furnace would soon come online, adding some capacity. But even the upgraded incinerator would still handle significantly less than the city's growing load.

As mayor, DelBello had enacted emergency legislation to reduce price-gouging for local businesses and raised the tipping fees for private carters. He ended the mob's control of the city's incinerator. But Croton was still the terminus for trash the city couldn't burn. Now that last refuge would close inside of a decade.

The federal government was pushing Martinelli for a solution. He wanted to turn the city's existing incinerator into its own waste-to-energy plant and recycling center. He and Republican council member Charles Cola were well aware of the county's desire to purchase the incinerator. It would relieve them of a hefty investment in upgrades but commit them to a higher disposal cost. Economically, it made perfect sense. But the mayor and the Republican-dominated council saw it as a power play by their former mayor.

The city's size gave it some swagger. Yonkers generated just under twenty-five percent of Westchester's annual load of 900,000 tons per year. That meant shelling out more than $3 million per year if it joined the county plan. But the city was already spending half of that collecting and processing its own trash. Cola argued that the upgraded city-owned plant would save municipal money by heating public buildings. Yonkers might be able to sell excess electricity on the private market. He estimated the final post-market disposal cost at $4.50 per ton – an unlikely prediction that would soon double.

The city's capital investment to upgrade the plant could cost $16 million. DelBello urged the council to reconsider, arguing that the county could retrofit the plant for two-thirds of that amount at its own expense. The only cost to the city would be the $15-per-ton tipping fee. The deal would cancel the city's planned debt and possibly produce an immediate windfall. The city balked.

Yonkers wasn't alone in hesitating. The Republican mayor of Mount Vernon, August Petrillo, was stalling DelBello. His city wanted to build a new municipal plant using Union Carbide's "Purox" system, an advanced digester that converts trash to burnable fuel. Petrillo believed his plant would be far more efficient than the county's incinerator, making that system obsolete. But the Purox design was still highly experimental. The company had only a working prototype. Ironically, DelBello wanted to proceed with the very same Purox system in Mount Vernon. But it would be paid for by the county, and if it had problems, trash could easily be transferred to another county incinerator. Despite the obvious benefit to Mount Vernon, the turf war persisted.

By summer 1974, New Rochelle and White Plains verbally agreed to support the county's proposal. The board of legislators voted 16-0 in favor of the county trash plan. Still, Yonkers wanted to go it alone. Cola, believing the state would cost-share the new Yonkers facility, estimated disposal costs could be as low as $1 to $2 per ton. DelBello was worried that this kind of showboating by Yonkers and Mount Vernon might sway other local governments away from the solid waste proposal. Some incinerator companies, seeing an opportunity, tried to sweet-talk municipalities into private deals. Fortunately, most of those deals were declined.

By September, news began to leak that the Yonkers City Council had been presented with a bill for $250,000 – an initial payment for several million dollars of work done earlier to bring the existing incinerator up to 1968 standards. Millions more were in the pipeline to meet current federal rules. The council sheepishly referred the invoice to a committee. The newspapers asked why – especially after a financial scandal involving recent incinerator improvements – did the city still owe this money? And why had the city shunned the county plan for the better part of a year if joining the regional plan would have paid off the debt and eliminated the need for future fixes? It was an embarrassment.

In that same month, the county submitted its preliminary plan to the state DEC. The document was needed to get the state funding ball rolling. Yonkers feigned outrage, perhaps to distract public focus from its own financial bungling. Cola sent a letter directly to the DEC complaining that they never formally agreed to anything. But no one had. It was a plan, not a contract – a prerequisite to access tens of millions of dollars in state funding. Most locally elected officials enthusiastically supported the county's submission. The county board of legislators had unanimously voted in favor of the plan several months earlier. The state DEC viewed the regional effort favorably. No other town complained – except Mount Vernon.

Cola sent a copy of his letter to Mayor Petrillo to gin up a down-county Republican revolt. Petrillo fired off an identical letter of protest, giving new meaning to "trash talk." Though the two towns together represented one-third of the county's garbage load, DelBello knew he could exclude them if they desired. The final county waste plan was approved by the board of legislators for $105.7 million. The county applied to the state for $52 million in funding. It still included all county municipalities. Yonkers and Mount Vernon could exclude themselves later if they so desired. DelBello hoped they wouldn't.

By February 1975, Yonkers' deficit had ballooned to $3.7 million. Its incinerator had long been out of federal air quality compliance. It was under a DEC mandate to decide on much-delayed plant improvements. Thousands of dollars in federal fines were racking up. A month later, the council stunningly voted for two opposing plans at the same meeting – one to join with the county and one to continue to build its own plant. Both would languish. At one point, DelBello presented the city with a written proposal, supported by Yonkers City Manager

Emmet Casey, to pay $3.5 million in county funds for the city's incinerator and facilities. It would instantly have canceled the city's trash-related debt. But Martinelli had refused to sign, claiming the need to explore other options. Casey was unequivocal. "Our city is not in a position to have funds for a thermal plant," he stated flatly.

Mount Vernon, while not in a fiscal hole like Yonkers, still had a difficult budgetary challenge. Its garbage-related taxes comprised a whopping nine percent of the city's budget. Finding an affordable solid waste alternative was critical. Because of delays in the plant's planned construction and the uncertainty surrounding the Purox system, funding from the state was in jeopardy. The untested technology, long advocated by Petrillo, had now risen from $4 million to $6 million. Eventually, it would rise to $12 million. Incredulously, he claimed "the county isn't doing anything" to help when DelBello had been banging on his door for a year.

He was ready to give up on Yonkers and Mount Vernon. But he felt he had a "moral obligation" to include them. He would scale back the project only if he had to. Ironically, a smaller plant might be slightly more beneficial for county finances by lowering bond-funded debt. But having the county's two biggest cities in an economic crisis over garbage plans could trash their municipal bond rating. That would be bad for Westchester.

In 1975, with Yonkers on the edge of financial default, an angry electorate installed a Democratic majority on the council, isolating Martinelli. The council abandoned the city's unlikely plans for its own incinerator and switched to a county transfer station on an interim basis. It would formally sign up with the county weeks before its 1979 sink-or-swim deadline. Mount Vernon relented as well after Petrillo died of an apparent heart attack in August 1976. The two cities put the county over the finish line in terms of generating enough garbage – 400,000 tons per year – to make the energy plant operative.

Soon things were looking bright for the county's trash dilemma. In the first half of 1975, DelBello reached a settlement agreement on the Croton Point federal lawsuit. The landfill would stay open until 1981. The top of the fill would be graded, capped and sealed to prevent further leaching into the Hudson. A revenue-generating golf course and park were considered as a permanent public reuse of the site.

More good news came in August. The state awarded Westchester $42.5 million for a countywide solid waste system. It was forty percent of the total cost of the thirty-year project. DelBello was beaming: "Ours is the only real regional program in the state." Though designs had begun, DelBello gave Yonkers additional time. Things were not moving as fast as expected on the county plant. In the end, the extended timeline would help him. With the U.S. still feeling the effects of the 1973–74 OPEC oil embargo, alternative energy was becoming the hottest ticket in town.

Enter Con Ed

DelBello thought back to his appeal to Con Edison several years earlier. DelBello met with Charles Luce, the utility's CEO. At that time, DelBello was considering a scaled-down plant that would create a thermal output but leave the energy generation to the utility. They thought Con Ed would be thrilled and would build a new energy turbine on the same site.

No dice. Luce had no interest in investing in, owning, or operating any power-generating equipment. Instead, he wanted to purchase the power the county generated at a wholesale price and resell it to customers. That was a non-starter for DelBello:

"I invited Charles Luce to my office to discuss the waste-to-energy process. I offered to provide the steam or heat output from a plant the county would build. Luce only had to build the electric generation end of the process. He said 'no' on the spot."

But when the county's plans for the plant firmed up, Con Ed became worried Westchester was moving in on its turf. At the end of 1978, it abruptly reversed itself. Suddenly, Con Ed wanted to build a $50-million-dollar waste-to-energy plant. Nevertheless, DelBello moved forward with the referendum authorizing the county to take over Con Ed's energy generation and distribution network. The county's plans continued to move forward.

Peekskill to the rescue

By 1979, another federal regulation came down the pike which looked more like an opportunity than a burden, and DelBello was ready. Ocean dumping of sewage sludge – the detritus left over from the wastewater treatment process – had become a national environmental issue. New federal regulations would prohibit it, starting in 1981. DelBello knew the incinerator would burn almost anything while scrubbing ninety-five percent of the pollutants from the waste. Why not sewage? The county's annual load of 60,000 tons of nitrogen-rich sludge would be more fuel for the fire and a cheap means of disposal. While other jurisdictions up and down the Eastern Seaboard scrambled to find expensive alternatives to ocean dumping, DelBello was already turning regulations into revenue.

But trouble was brewing in Valhalla. The use of the

Grasslands Reservation for the county's waste-to-energy plant was now in question. Despite the substantial size of the county site and its co-location with the new, burgeoning Westchester Medical Center, residents of Mount Pleasant – the town in which the village of Valhalla is located – were up in arms that "a garbage dump" would be located in their area. Encouraged by Edward J. Brady, a Republican Mount Pleasant representative on the board of legislators, the objection gathered steam. With the Grasslands Reservation housing a 600-bed hospital, medical school, New York Medical College, and a county jail wedged between two major highways, the idea of a high-tech trash incinerator seemed too much for the community to bear. DelBello needed another location for the plant.

Peekskill stepped into Valhalla's shoes. The city of Peekskill was eager to host the new trash-to-energy plant. Unlike Valhalla, Peekskill didn't have the convenience of a center-county location, but the city wanted to be the centerpiece of the county's bold, new energy plan. It lies on the edge of the Hudson River in Westchester's northwest corner, roughly eight miles upstream from Croton Point. At the time, Peekskill was in financial trouble. One of its best sources of revenue, the Standard Brands Co., had closed shop three years earlier. Several other smaller employers had left as well. It had trouble attracting new business to the sixty-five-acre site – primarily because of high utility costs, as was true in much of the county.

With Peekskill in play, Westchester could bring in a huge source of tax revenue and cheap power to attract other businesses. The city also had something essential for a power plant – nearby access to the electrical grid. A major substation serving the aging Indian Point nuclear power plant was a mere mile away.

But the proposed site was not on county land. At Grasslands, the county could build whatever its voters approved. Any municipality in Westchester could participate. The county could establish the payment terms for municipal use of the plant. But because the Peekskill site was not on county land, a formal agreement was needed to give the county control over the facility and to contract with other municipalities. Establishing a "solid waste district" was one method already available under state law. But that law stipulated the levying of a tax on each town to finance operations, rather than using the more incentive-oriented "pay-as-you-throw" fee of $15 per ton that DelBello had envisioned. A per capita tax payment had political baggage and would have reduced the incentive for recycling.

There was a way around this. If participating towns were to sign an "inter-municipal agreement," the county could avoid the one-price-fits-all tax levy. But it would require a special county referendum. The timing turned out to be advantageous. In 1979, after years of being held captive by Con Edison's sky-high electricity prices, DelBello had moved forward with a referendum that would free the county to form its own public utility, compete with Con Edison for cheaper hydropower and even allow the county to buy out most of its transmission and distribution facilities. It was a potentially expensive proposal, but it could work. Con Ed fought the referendum in a $1.3 million media campaign that claimed the county would go broke – a false notion, given that it only gave the county the power to take over electrical distribution and facilities with the board of legislators' approval. Nevertheless, the referendum was defeated. Though the idea of a county-owned and operated utility was gone, it would garner national media attention for its innovation.

After the defeat, DelBello said he would drop further public utility efforts. But many people, even those who had opposed his specific proposal, were still concerned about Con Edison's high-priced monopoly. Once DelBello realized that creating an inter-municipal agreement for the Peekskill waste-to-energy plant was needed, he thought that modifying his original referendum might get it passed. If he could get Con Ed to approve a scaled-down public utility option, he could – in typical DelBello fashion – kill two birds with one stone.

By early 1982, the board of legislators had approved two related referendums for county voters. Proposition 1, more modest than his referendum two years earlier, would establish a Public Utility Service Agency (PUSA) that could buy power elsewhere and negotiate with Con Ed to use some of its distribution and transmission facilities. This meant that Westchester could buy cheap hydroelectric power from PASNY, while the grid infrastructure would remain in Con Edison's hands. Con Ed expressed no opposition to the referendum. It passed five to one.

Proposition 2 was essential to the success of the Peekskill waste-to-energy plant. It set up a special taxing district for the plant's thirty-five participating Westchester communities. The agreement avoided both the time and expense of establishing a solid waste district and the politically unappealing per capita tax payment from the municipalities. Instead, they would pay a $17-per-ton tipping fee with a five-year price lock. As part of the referendum, the towns agreed to sign "put-or-pay" contracts, promising delivery of minimum garbage volumes to avoid paying fines, thereby discouraging side-contracts with private vendors. The referendum was so critical that Wheelabrator Frye, the plant's chosen manufacturer and operator, held off on construction until the voters passed it – which they did, with a comfortable three-to-one margin.

Peekskill's mayor, Fred J. "Jay" Bianco, was ecstatic. He noted, "Not counting the allied industry the facility might draw, this plant could initially pay some $2.3 million in (local) tax dollars in the first year and ultimately some $5 million annually." The actual benefit would later be a rate decline of

$1 million – about 12.5% of its annual energy costs as a city. It would also get payments of $1.5 million in lieu of taxes. By 2009, that number had risen to $7 million. The plant would quickly resolve the city's financial problems and attract additional businesses as a result of lower energy costs.

By the time of the plant's christening in 1984, it had grown in scale from its modest thirty-five-megawatt design to a sixty-megawatt behemoth. Wheelabrator Frye had decided to forgo producing steam for municipal heat due to the plant's isolated location. Instead, it focused solely on generating electricity for 55,000 homes by incinerating 2,250 tons of municipal solid waste and sewage sludge each day. A negative pressure ventilation system kept the plant's odiferous operations contained on the site. Because of the extensive recycling system DelBello had built in Westchester, the remaining trash load was reduced in volume by ninety percent, with the resulting ash carted away by the operating company. Even Con Ed finally got involved, purchasing and distributing all of the plant's electricity. The total value of the energy was close to $20 million per year. After debt service and payouts to Peekskill, the county was optimistic about seeing a net profit in five to seven years.

There were delays and changes in the original plan over the years. The disposal cost increased from $15 to $17 per ton to address America's rising inflation from high fuel prices. It was still a bargain, given that landfills were closing and federal laws on solid waste and air pollution were tightening. The closure of the Croton landfill was extended to 1986 to allow the county time to finish building the facility. Ultimately, the site became Croton Point Park, a premier recreation area with restored wetlands and magnificent views of the more pristine Hudson River.

DelBello smiled when remembering his mayoral years, fighting to reclaim the city's incinerator and its garbage collection services from the mob, the issue itself a metaphoric battle against Yonkers' endemic crime. Here he was a decade later, the county executive of Westchester, once again dealing with trash, this time on a regional scale. The metaphor endured. He was, in his own estimation, "Mr. Clean-Up," the sanitationist of society, the street sweeper of crime, the property manager of Westchester's landscape. He saw alternatives to landfills when landfills were being closed. He saw garbage as fuel when fuel prices were rising. He saw an economic opportunity when others saw only despair. He had a remarkable political and social clairvoyance that evaded other politicians. His political life was a never-ending flow of problems and challenges to be sorted, prioritized and processed, creating new energy and wealth for a growing, dynamic county.

CHAPTER 12

A New Hospital for Westchester

"Not on your life," an angry doctor shouted from the audience.

"Why not?" DelBello shouted back, baiting the doctor.

"Because we have patients, and you don't."

In a sense, the doctor was right. DelBello had lost his "patience."

It was one of several unnerving private meetings between the county administration and doctors. The doctor was joined by roughly forty other physicians who objected to the new Westchester Medical Center in Valhalla, where the decaying Grasslands Hospital had stood for decades. The new hospital would deliver "tertiary" care – highly specialized, cutting-edge medicine that had previously been available only in New York City or Albany. It would be a teaching hospital affiliated with the New York Medical College, which would likely attract research funds and renowned medical professionals. Local hospitals throughout Westchester, and in surrounding counties, including Dutchess, Rockland, Orange and Ulster, had always referred difficult medical cases to New York's two major cities. Now they had another option, one that could save time – and thus, lives.

The doctors are out

But the doctors were wary. Despite the preeminence of a high-quality teaching hospital, they worried the new center would rob the local hospitals where they had maintained admitting privileges for decades of less urgent-care patients. Many of these hospitals were already economically stressed. They thought the new medical center would drive them out of business.

DelBello assured them that wouldn't happen. The purpose of the new medical center was to make Westchester a destination for those complicated cases local hospitals couldn't treat – burns, cancers, problematic pregnancies, rare childhood diseases. He pointed out that their repeated attempts to block tertiary care would force the medical center to compete with surrounding hospitals on more typical secondary cases – a self-defeating response that would cost local doctors the very patients they didn't want to lose.

It was the fall of 1976, two months before the medical center was scheduled to open. The county was $61 million in debt, an intentional financing gamble that would pay off handsomely. But DelBello was one of the few who knew that. He also knew that an interdisciplinary medical center was essential to the vitality of one of the country's most important, powerful counties – an institution as important to the healthy as to the sick.

The idea of building a tertiary-care teaching hospital had been on the county's agenda for a decade. In the late 1960s, then county executive Ed Michaelian had proposed an upgrade of the Grasslands Reservation. It was a spacious site established in 1915 to house less desirable public health services far from populated areas. Conceived as an almshouse and a hospital for indigent patients, the isolated Grasslands was ideal for treating patients with dangerous communicable diseases – tuberculosis, polio, scarlet fever, and diphtheria. As medicine modernized and the population grew, new hospital construction throughout the county made the Grasslands Reservation a dumping ground for the indigent and poor.

Deficiencies multiplied. There was little inventory control. Containers of medications frequently disappeared. Undercover police raided the pathology lab. An investigation revealed the hospital had been used for private practices. Two doctors were arrested and charged with fraud.

Wanting to leave a legacy, Michaelian quickly assembled a deal in which the county would put up $28 million for a new, state-of-the-art hospital. New York Medical College would raise an additional $23 million and erect several academic buildings. Westchester voters approved the $28 million bond program. The county secured a $61 million loan from the state for the cost of construction, keeping the unused bonds as a backup. It would need it.

The deal with the medical college was flawed. Though Westchester taxpayers were responsible for the majority of the center's funding, the college retained management and spending authority. There were no clear contingencies stipulating what would happen if the college's part of the deal fell through. And that is exactly what occurred.

In March 1973, as construction was underway, it became apparent that the medical college would not be able to raise its $23 million share. Instead, it arranged for a loan from a consortium of banks. But the loan was conditioned on the college having dibs on future hospital revenues. This put

Westchester taxpayers on the hook for paying off the state loans while being shunted to the back of the line for revenues. The agreement became the county G.O.P.'s white elephant.

Nine months later, when DelBello became county executive, he knew that the otherwise praiseworthy hospital project needed financial restructuring. He insisted that if the medical college were not responsible for building the hospital or sharing the deficit, it shouldn't have any control over management – or revenues. DelBello orchestrated a new affiliation agreement. The county would assume full control of the medical center, and the medical college would provide health services while continuing its teaching program.

In May 1975, the county and the New York Medical College signed a revised agreement. County Commissioner of Hospitals and Medical Director Joseph A. Cimino, M.D., was appointed to run the center. Although the county was now on the hook for all the financing, it had complete control. It was still a daunting financial burden, but DelBello knew he could manage it.

A regional hospital

Well before his county executive election, DelBello had advocated for a state-of-the-art regional hospital. He envisioned the medical center as the main component of a seven-county health care system, one that would compete with New York City and Albany but not smaller local hospitals. At DelBello's urging, the county executives of Dutchess and Putnam joined him in his quest for a regional medical center.

The venture required support from the federal government, however, as the Department of Health, Education and Welfare had not formally established the separate mid-Hudson health region that DelBello envisioned. He would need

**DelBello greeting President-elect Jimmy Carter in
New York City.**

that federal support to assist him in developing a multi-service
regional hospital. Having been President Jimmy Carter's first
elected supporter in New York State, DelBello met with the
new president to ask for his help. Carter directed him to Patri-
cia Roberts Harris, secretary of Health, Education and Welfare (now Health and Human Services), resulting in the
establishment of a new mid-Hudson region, with the new
Westchester Medical Center as its tertiary-care facility.

This was about more than good medicine. Westchester
was growing. The medical profession was expanding. Advanced medical care would attract business investment. It
would create ancillary medical jobs, boost in-county medical
education and make Westchester an even more desirable place
to live. The medical center wasn't simply an amenity. It was a
strategic investment in the county's future – and a visionary

example of supply begetting demand.

But DelBello had to assuage smaller hospitals, whose affiliated physicians were understandably nervous. They thought the new medical center would be a drain on the region's medical network of doctors and patients for common conditions like obstetrics and broken bones. DelBello understood that the hospital would be successful – and acceptable – only if it provided cutting-edge medical science not otherwise available within the county.

There was still the issue of the deficit. DelBello was certain he could get the medical center's finances back in the black. Then it could be turned over to the private sector. He saw the county as an incubator for premier medical services that eventually would transfer to private operations. The county might break even, but the economic and social legacy of having spawned an advanced medical center start-up would echo throughout the county for decades. Westchester's citizens would be able to access top-notch care, attracting more wealth, more jobs, and more cross-sector investments in high-tech and knowledge-based industries.

He needed a few years to make the hospital financially solvent. The new facility had to be stabilized. A positive revenue stream would depend in large part on the cooperation of the existing medical community to fill patient beds willingly. Without local referrals and top-flight doctors to run new programs, the private sector wouldn't bite, and the deficit would drag on.

With a little more than a year to go before opening, financial trouble arose. The state's Housing Finance Agency, which funded construction, began to fall behind on its payments to the county. The state was over-obligated with construction projects. Contractors temporarily walked off the job, although the construction was still well ahead of schedule.

DelBello saw this as a stroke of luck. He had been frustrated by the state's high interest costs. The county had recently earned a triple-A bond rating, the result of his tight fiscal management in a time of national economic distress. It could issue its own debt at rates significantly lower than the outstanding state bonds. At DelBello's urging, the board of legislators requested higher bonding authority from the state legislature. The state senate's majority leader, Republican Warren Anderson, trusted DelBello's sense of finance and arranged for a vote to approve the request. The low-interest county bonds saved Westchester $40 million in interest costs over the thirty-year life of the loan and kept its triple-A bond rating intact.

Yet the board of legislators – the ones who had enthusiastically supported Michaelian's original proposal and had just endorsed DelBello's bonding authority increase – were now becoming skittish. Several members griped about Westchester absorbing so much debt. County taxpayers were on the hook for a $13 million deficit in the first year of operation. Doctors and regional hospital administrators were unhappy. The board was getting heat from all sides.

Ed Brady, the board's Republican chairman, tried to take a scalpel to the hospital's plans. He proposed a resolution to limit the hospital's expansion to a mere replacement of the older facility. Forget tertiary care, he argued. We can't afford it and we won't get the business.

This call to inaction would have halted hiring medical staff and the purchase of essential equipment until the county "made up its mind." Doctors and hospital administrators, fearing that the new hospital wouldn't attract tertiary-care patients, went back to their old arguments and lined up behind Brady, inadvertently advocating the competitive glut of common care they most feared. But the public was too far down the road to turn back. It trusted DelBello, who responded in a cooperative letter explaining the hospital's purpose and addressing the board's concerns. The resolution ultimately failed.

Grand opening

The hospital opened in March 1977 with DelBello strolling through the seven-story structure nestled between the Saw Mill and Sprain Brook parkways. The views from the upper-floor suites were stunning. Elegant semiprivate rooms were decorated with framed murals. TV monitors on rocker arms sprung like modern art from the freshly painted pastel walls. Nursing stations glowed with lights and call buttons. Medical professionals in blue scrubs efficiently paced the shining linoleum hallways. There was a persistent, soft hum of anti-septic ventilation and medical electronics, punctuated by the pulse of beeping monitors and the persistent hiss of oxygen lines.

DelBello visiting one of the hospital labs at the new Westchester Medical Center.

Only half of the hospital's 511 beds were open. Joe Cimino had conveyed, to the consternation of uninformed critics, that the hospital would not be full for four years. He and DelBello knew that this was the nature of a medical start-up. You had to build capacity slowly and sequentially, lest there be nothing concrete or organized to sell to the top medical professionals you were trying to attract. It was, as DelBello stated, "the most modern hospital between New York City and Albany." The hospital itself was a standing advertisement for medical excellence to attract more medical excellence. That's what it needed.

Some doctors still dragged their feet – especially obstetricians worried that their most important sources of revenue would be depleted. DelBello convinced them that only high-risk obstetrics patients would be treated there, a service the local hospitals didn't deliver. He noted that roughly 200 women from Westchester had to go to New York City each year because they couldn't be treated by county hospitals. "What about the mothers?" he asked. "Will they prefer making trips into Manhattan rather than coming to a new facility in the center of the county?" Slowly, the doctors relented.

A year after opening, the hospital was operating at seventy-one percent capacity, a promising statistic. The CAT scanner – a revolutionary technology at the time that crafted three-dimensional landscapes of the body's interior – was booked. So was catheterization, a lifesaving means of snaking diagnostic tubes through the body's vessels. The hospital had hired one of the country's renowned neurosurgeons, Irving Cooper, M.D., who had revolutionized cryogenic brain surgery. He brought with him twenty-five to thirty patients a month and a stream of government and private grants.

The hospital also hired George Reed, M.D., a nationally celebrated specialist in open-heart surgery. Reed, a college fencing champion, exchanged his foil for a scalpel. He had earned a doctorate in veterinary medicine and served in the U.S. Army, performing the first open-heart surgeries on animals – a proving ground for his career in human cardiology. He returned to the New York University Grossman School of Medicine for his medical degree, became a cardiac surgeon, and performed the first human open-heart surgery in 1959. His practice expanded over time to include cardiac bypass, valve repair and the use of frozen, preserved tissue in operations. Before Reed arrived, the medical center was performing fifty open-heart surgeries per year. By 1980, that number had risen to 600 – a testament to the importance of the doctor's medical reputation.

Yet the medical center's operating deficit was still climbing, partly due to inefficient third-party billing practices. DelBello brought in Bernard M. Weinstein as the county's commissioner of hospitals. Weinstein had earned kudos running Bellevue Hospital in Manhattan. He knew that the hospital would succeed by providing services that weren't otherwise available in Westchester. The best doctors and surgeons would make the hospital a financial magnet. Weinstein's tenure confirmed what DelBello had long argued – that excellent health care and an improving fiscal status would make it easier for the county to get out of the hospital business. By the end of the second year of operation, the open beds had an outstanding eighty-two percent occupancy rate – although only sixty percent of all beds were operational. Weinstein said that they might make a profit when they opened the remaining beds.

The board of legislators was skeptical. After some heated discussion, DelBello agreed to sell the hospital if deficits climbed beyond $14 million after the second year of operation. He was confident the center would come in under that mark.

He also knew that the hospital needed more time to develop its reputation to become financially sound. That would make it a more valuable, saleable asset.

He was right on both counts. A combination of more efficient billing and excellent marketing drew attention and money to the hospital. Deficits were lower than expected. In 1979, the hospital had turned a corner. Even financial skeptics on the board of legislators were coming around. Privatization of the hospital was now on the horizon. A deal would be several years off, giving the county more time to shrink deficits and expand sorely needed services.

Specialties for a special place

One of the great strengths of an interdisciplinary medical center was units devoted to particular illnesses or conditions. Of particular importance to Westchester was a burn center. Long advocated by DelBello, the burn center would treat patients who otherwise had to be sent out of the county. Many local leaders noted that Boston's burn center could save someone with burns over ninety-five percent of their body. But in these cases, time and expertise were of the essence. In Westchester, those patients wouldn't stand a chance.

This was personal to DelBello. Years earlier, a fire in his hometown of Yonkers had critically injured two children. They ultimately succumbed to their wounds because the care they needed wasn't available nearby. Jack S. Goldman, M.D., the county's commissioner of health, noted that more than 250 people were severely burned in fires and other incidents in Westchester each year. Goldman believed they deserved the best possible treatment – especially the firefighters who risked their lives every day to save others.

Since the beginning of his administration, DelBello fought for a burn center, working closely with several leading firefighters, including John Bogart of White Plains and Jack Williams of New Rochelle – himself a burn victim. With the endorsement of the county's firefighters' associations, they advocated for state legislation and funding. As early as April 1974, DelBello appointed a task force to coordinate a burn center plan. He was joined by a chorus of Democratic and Republican county politicians and state legislators to raise private funding for the unit at the Westchester Medical Center. He sought money from the state legislature and coordinated a "Burn Center Day" to raise funds.

The Burn Center opened in 1979. The ten-bed unit was a national model designed to treat the most severely burned patients. It was the only such center between New York City and Albany. The majority of patients with severe burns were the young and the elderly – individuals who most needed the support of families who might be unable to visit or stay with them in far-off locations. An extraordinary team of doctors, nurses, dieticians, students, therapists and housekeepers worked with the patients to stop infections, treat pain and deal with the psychological trauma of disfigurement. The burn unit also conducted research and provided therapy to help burn patients return to work.

In 1980, the hospital opened the long-awaited Westchester Cancer Screening Center. Prior to its opening, the majority of cancer cases were treated at other local hospitals. The most challenging cancer cases were referred to New York City. To run the new center, the hospital recruited Roy Ashikari, M.D., a prominent breast cancer specialist from Memorial Sloan Kettering in Manhattan.

Both doctors and patients were eager to be part of West-chester's new cancer center. Leukemia therapies, bone-marrow transplants and other highly advanced cancer treatments were all housed at the center. DelBello referred to Ashikari as a "star." He understood that advanced medicine and patients followed the most renowned doctors. Having that provider's care closer to home, especially in matters of life and death, made eminent sense.

In subsequent years, the hospital opened a high-risk perinatal center, a neurosurgery unit, a geriatrics facility and a therapy center for the developmentally disabled. Each center attracted the next one as the hospital's high-quality, interdisciplinary reputation continued to grow. The Maria Fareri Children's Hospital – although opened in 2004, twenty-two years after DelBello's time as county executive – was housed at the Westchester Medical Center because patients and doctors had access to so many other related specialties that already existed. Named after a thirteen-year-old girl who had died from rabies, the Maria Fareri center was built through the intensive fundraising of her parents, Brenda and John Fareri. Their daughter had passed away at a hospital that wasn't geared toward children, with no room for parents to attend to their children. They made sure the new center had large private rooms to accommodate families, with access to aquariums, music, toys, and art.

By the end of 1982, DelBello's last year as county executive, the hospital's annual deficit had fallen by nearly half of the amount that had existed five years earlier. Nearly two-thirds of the patients were from the county and roughly one-third from the surrounding six-county area in the Hudson Valley. As opposition to the medical center evaporated, local hospitals in the seven-county area were transferring over 2,000 patients per year to the medical center.

The hospital went through some difficult financial periods in the late 1990s and early 2000s, with plans for a shutdown because of a rising deficit. But the doctors, nurses, technicians and maintenance staff still showed up without pay. They had become wedded to the medical center. It had become more than a hospital. It was a devotion. Some debt restructuring, fundraising and a final, full transfer to a private nonprofit entity resuscitated the center. Today it thrives, performing procedures that are unique within the Hudson Valley, such as using TransMedics' "Heart-in-a-Box" to allow for a greater pool of viable hearts in transplant surgery; and Gamma Tile, an implanted, time-release form of radiation that can mitigate the stress of postoperative therapy for those who have undergone the removal of cancerous brain tumors.

DelBello understood that a county like Westchester would be enriched by a multifaceted health care and research institution. Its voracious demand for knowledge and information grew tendrils in nearby educational institutions. Its technology birthed clusters of medical jobs throughout the county. Its reputation implanted growing companies whose employees wanted a reputable medical center in their backyards. Like a beating heart, the medical center pumped the lifeblood of a vital, growing county.

But the story of a hospital isn't really about a hospital. It's not about the doctors. It's about the people healed within its walls. The same could be said of a visionary political leader, for such a leader is nothing more than a provider of services to the community that elected him, invested in him, trusted in him. DelBello's job was to make sure that the county remained healthy, that its prognosis was good and that it would lead a long, prosperous life. And like a compassionate doctor whose only concern was the health of the body politic, DelBello saw to it that the medical center was stabilized and got back up on its feet.

CHAPTER 13

Thinning the Blue Line

The frigid midnight air settled like a layer of ice on Valhalla's Grasslands Reservation in February 1981. In the winter chill, a member of DelBello's staff jangled keys, searching for the one that would open the door to Thomas Delaney's office, the sheriff and public safety commissioner whose accusations and incompetence had become a black mark against DelBello's administration.

The knob turned. Several of his staff entered the office, flashlights slicing the dark and glinting off the brushed filing cabinets. There they found a treasure trove of culpability – evidence of deputies promoted for political patronage, notes detailing the sheriff's obstruction of county management and campaign material supporting DelBello's opponent, State Senator Joseph R. Pisani, in the upcoming November election. The searchers double-padlocked the door to prevent Delaney or any of his police associates from trying to reclaim materials. He would be formally suspended later that morning.

The "Monday Morning Massacre" – DelBello's sobriquet for the raid, named after the 1973 "Saturday Night Massacre," Nixon's retaliatory response to the Watergate investigation – was, in his view, a necessary action to remove a perpetual roadblock to the unification of policing under one agency. Before DelBello took office, policing had been split between two county departments. The sheriff's office was Westchester's first police agency, dating back two-and-a-half centuries. It had functioned independently since its inception. As the county's top cop, the sheriff answered to the voters who elected him. Although the office occasionally assisted local police, it focused primarily on countywide crimes. The sheriff also had a fleet of marine enforcement boats, as Westchester – nestled between the Long Island Sound and the Hudson River – was a magnet for water-borne drug trafficking.

A tale of two police forces

The Parkway Police was a department of county government. Created in the late 1920s to patrol Westchester's newly built motorways, the Parkway Police handled traffic problems, investigated crimes on county property and tackled welfare fraud. This department also had detectives and a small marine unit and supervised Westchester's only bomb squad. As could be expected, there was a significant amount of uncoordinated, duplicate effort between the two agencies – booking systems, dispatchers, vehicles, filing systems and so on. There was also some mutual suspicion.

DelBello knew the county would benefit socially and financially by integrating its police departments. He hadn't always felt that way. As mayor of Yonkers, he had been opposed to the idea of merging the sheriff's office and the Parkway Police.

Ed Michaelian, his county executive predecessor, had proposed a unified police force under county administration. He had had a dispute with the sheriff at that time, Republican Daniel McMahon, over trying to control personnel costs through a wage settlement package for the Civil Service Employees Association. McMahon was fuming that the county executive dared to include county employees in a settlement agreement. He flatly opposed Michaelian's pitch for a unified police department. The proposal died in committee at the board of legislators.

In 1973, when DelBello was running for county executive, he was approached by a Yonkers' Republican district leader while campaigning on the city's Sadore Lane. As the two chatted amicably, the district leader offered a revelatory comment.

"I've been told that if I hold your numbers down in this district, Delaney will make me deputy sheriff when he gets elected," he exclaimed proudly. How would that be accomplished? What gave Delaney the right to meddle in an election and a district leader the knowledge or experience to be a deputy sheriff for Westchester County? More disturbing to DelBello was that he and Delaney weren't even running for the same job. Yet Delaney was working to defeat him and get opponent Edward N. Vetrano elected as county executive to keep a Republican lock on county politics.

Antagonist in blue

On the surface, Delaney had a record as a decent cop and an admirable leader. He had served as a captain in New York City, his hometown, before becoming the commissioner of the Mount Vernon police department in 1968. But in 1975, after Delaney had become the Westchester County Sheriff, former

Mount Vernon Police Capt. Thomas Sharpe accused Delaney and Mayor August Petrillo of building an "aura of corruption" after the indictment of thirteen current and former city detectives. Sharpe, a seventeen-year veteran of the Mount Vernon police force, cited illegal gambling and favoritism in assignments and promotions. He specifically referenced two detectives who were demoted to uniform duty after arresting Carmine Tripodi, a known gambler who admitted giving bribes to cops. It demoralized honest cops and enticed dishonest ones. Sharpe made it clear that he would not support the administration's corruption. That put him on Petrillo's blacklist. Sharpe found that his schedule was being constantly switched, apparently as a form of harassment. He finally resigned.

It became clear to DelBello that the sheriff's office was corrupt and incompetent. Yet, at the same time, there were no guardrails against political malfeasance. A county executive candidate who promised to rein in irregularities in the sheriff's office might be politically doomed. He wondered: Could the sheriff's department raise slanderous accusations against him in a press conference? Could a sheriff go as far as manufacturing evidence against him? He would later find out. It was, as a board of legislators representative Audrey Hochsberg stated in a New York Times op-ed, "an unhealthy mixture of politics and police power."

Over the years, many county executives had complained about the sheriff's office, citing secrecy in budgeting, political patronage and obstinacy in coordinating the sheriff's staff with other county functions. Now DelBello understood why Michaelian's proposal made sense. If he won the county executive's seat, he would deal with this head on. In 1973, when DelBello was elected county executive for the first time, Delaney was elected county sheriff. From the beginning, Delaney knew DelBello was in favor of merging the two police departments, and he would have none of it. He was, as the Daily News reported, "itching for a confrontation." The two men would spar for much of the next decade.

Near the end of DelBello's first term, he proposed a unified county police department under the control of the county executive. The county budget justified his position. In the previous five years, the sheriff's allocation had increased by close to seventy-five percent, almost double the rate of increase for the Parkway Police and significantly more than the county as a whole. The national economy had suffered from rapid inflation in the middle of the decade. He had to bring police spending under control. A single police agency would ease the county's finances and address his concerns about uncontained political power in the sheriff's office.

Delaney also wanted a single county police force. But he wanted the Parkway Police under his authority. He had grown used to the idea of the voting public as his boss. He wasn't going to give that up. He was dead set against DelBello's plans from the get-go and ready to use any political weapon to maintain his power.

During the first two years of Delaney's tenure as sheriff, the district attorney had investigated allegations of financial misconduct in the sheriff's office. Though there were improprieties, the investigation didn't reveal any serious legal wrongdoing. Delaney blamed three "malcontents" on his staff and then shockingly claimed they were abetted by the county executive and county attorney, Gerry Harris. The district attorney refused to entertain the false accusation. DelBello and Harris were incensed.

When DelBello ran for re-election in 1977, Delaney again made news by railing against the Parkway Police. He claimed they were muscling in on the sheriff's criminal investigation and marine patrol activities. Carl Fulgenzi, the chief of the Parkway Police, flatly denied this. His agency already had a small marine unit with no plans for expansion. He noted that the Parkway Police were simply receiving more criminal investigation work within their jurisdiction.

For his part, Delaney was trying to quash the proposed merger. He thought the best way to do that was to cast a broad net of suspicion over DelBello's administration, hoping that it would derail his re-election. It didn't. He soundly defeated his Republican challenger, Gordon Burrows, whom the sheriff had openly supported.

Delaney on the attack

The election was barely over when Delaney filed a lawsuit against DelBello, claiming he used the 1978 budget "as a weapon" to punish him for his antipathy. The budget proposal requested a reduction in the sheriff's staff to increase the number of Parkway Police officers who were experiencing a higher work volume. But DelBello's budget could only suggest a decrease, as the sheriff's budget was handled separately by the board of legislators. If anything, it was a signal to the board that the merger should take place.

Delaney argued that an elected sheriff would be more independent and responsible to the voters. He claimed that a sheriff beholden to the county executive could easily be silenced through termination. But DelBello countered that reporting to the county executive would offer a more transparent view of police activities. The Board of Legislators would have the same budgetary discretion they always had. Voters would still have a voice at the ballot box if they were unhappy with any of the county executive's decisions, including his administration of the police.

The Board of Legislators wanted the merger. It would save

more than $1 million per year once the merger was in full swing. But the Republican majority was hesitant to step on one of their political allies. Delaney had been a devoted Republican. He held sway not only by virtue of his position but also by his political power. He could curry favor. And he was opposed to allowing DelBello to appoint his own commissioner to the new agency. One question remained: Who would control the new county police department – the sheriff or the county executive?

More wrangling ensued. Finally, DelBello compromised. Making Delaney the first commissioner of the new police force seemed like the only way through. He agreed to give Delaney an initial five-year appointment. The condition was added to the county bill. It was a devil's bargain in the short run, but it would make the police forever accountable to the county executive and the public, ending a long history of political wheeling and dealing reminiscent of DelBello's early days in Yonkers politics. It was the smart, professional thing to do. Besides, he thought, protecting Delaney might subdue the man's hostilities.

In July 1978, the board of legislators brought forward two referenda to create a unified Department of Public Safety Services in Westchester County. Both bills would merge the two countywide police forces into a single agency. But one bill designated the commissioner as a county executive appointee while the other called for a commissioner-by-election – essentially, a punt. For DelBello, the board's indecision emulated the legislative dithering that had infected the Yonkers City Council during the interminable debate over joining the county's trash program. No other commissioner working for a Westchester County agency was elected. Why should this department be any different? Fortunately, DelBello had enough votes on the board to sustain a veto. He killed the commissioner-by-vote proposal. The referendum authorizing the county executive to appoint the commissioner would be on the ballot in November.

On November 6, just one day before the election, deputy sheriffs working at the county courthouse staged a large and vocal protest. Most other political and law enforcement associations were in favor of the bill, including the Parkway Police Benevolent Association, the Tri-County Police Federation and the State Division of Criminal Justice Services. The political end-run demonstrated even more convincingly why a unified county-controlled police department was needed. Voters handily approved the bill by a two-to-one margin.

The new Department of Public Safety Services was scheduled to begin operations early in 1979. The merger would take several years to complete. Switchboards, filing systems, police stations, payroll and bookings were still separate and would have to be stitched together. Still, DelBello expected large savings in the first year of operation. What he didn't expect was that Delaney's crew would stand in his way.

Several weeks later, a group of the sheriff's deputies – many of the same ones who had protested the county bill the day before the election – filed a motion to suspend the new department because they feared losing their standing as court officers. In February, a state court judge invalidated part of the county law because it was being implemented before Delaney's previously elected term as sheriff was up. The commissioner-to-be remained the sheriff. The finding was upheld by a narrow vote in the Supreme Court of the State of New York. But the New York Court of Appeals – the highest court in the state – unanimously vacated that finding and reinstated the merger, ruling that the home-rule powers that gave Westchester the right to create the post also gave the county the right to abolish it. DelBello said that the favorable home-rule decision "shows there are still some ways of streamlining government."

In July 1979, Delaney was finally sworn in for a five-year term as the commissioner and sheriff – a dual appellation that would expire in several years. Carl Fulgenzi, the former chief of the Parkway Police, became deputy commissioner, as did the former undersheriff, Jack O'Brien. DelBello knew there would be conflicts, but as had always been the case, the betterment of Westchester County government was at stake. If Delaney could do the job, he would be satisfied.

L'affaire Bloomingdale's

But Delaney wasn't. Months later, a senior manager from Bloomingdale's White Plains had boarded a plane at Westchester County Airport without a ticket and refused to get off. County police arrested her. The woman became combative, claiming she was "friends" with DelBello and his wife Dee, the store's regional public relations director. It was a desperate, name-dropping attempt to try and avoid arrest. Deputy Police Commissioner Fulgenzi called DelBello to inform him. He, in turn, instructed Fulgenzi to follow standard procedures to the letter of the law. That should have been the end of the matter.

It wasn't. Delaney, smelling smoke, leapt into the fray, looking for fire. He accused DelBello in the press of interfering with police business and working on the sly with his own deputy commissioner to bury the matter. He said he had received an "anonymous" letter accusing them of secretly letting Bloomingdale's manager off the hook because of her connections. DelBello was livid. He directed his executive officer, Bob Dolan, to call Delaney and find out what "evidence" he had linking him to the alleged favoritism. He responded – again in the press – that the two had "no managerial authority" in the matter. Dolan, holding back laughter, told the papers that "something must have caused him to forget that he is no longer the elected sheriff of the county and is subject to the authority of the county executive."

This was enough for DelBello. Unable to get any cooperation from Delaney's office, he referred the case to Carl Vergari, the district attorney. He would like to have handled the matter without legal proceedings, but Delaney made that impossible. DelBello felt more comfortable with the matter in the D.A.'s hands. It relieved him of even the appearance of a cover-up and put the merits of the charge into a dispassionate court. Vergari appointed a grand jury to hear the case.

But DelBello was playing his cards close to the vest. He had plans for Delaney. Six months later, he convened a "blue ribbon" task force to examine why the merger of the two police agencies was still incomplete. Rules and regulations to guide the unified agency were never developed. The merging of equipment, support personnel and procedures had been delayed. Delaney called it a "kangaroo court." But the stall was intentional. In July 1980, Delaney had even threatened to derail the merger and obstruct DelBello's chance for re-election if he didn't extend his term of service by two years.

Eight months later, after the early morning seizure of Delaney's county office, DelBello filed formal charges against him. Delaney responded that he was being suspended because of the grand jury investigation regarding Bloomingdale's executive – the investigation that DelBello himself had asked Vergari to take over. DelBello had specifically held off on filing personnel charges against Delaney until Vergari gave him the all-clear that it wouldn't interfere with the grand jury inquiry. The timing was perfect.

There were some minor setbacks. A judge invalidated the suspension because Delaney hadn't been served a written notice of the charges, so he could respond. But the suspension wasn't a punishment – at least not yet. It was still an investigation. In this case, the person being investigated was the chief county law enforcement officer, someone with direct control over legal evidence. Suspension was essential. Delaney was still receiving pay and benefits. The Appeals Court, understanding the critical nature of this type of case, overruled the lower court's decision. DelBello moved forward. If dismissal were warranted, he would still have to go to the board of legislators to secure Delaney's removal.

Throughout his suspension, Delaney kept on the attack. He accused DelBello of inappropriately using county security to transport New York Yankees slugger Reggie Jackson to Bloomingdale's. (DelBello had, but while it may have had the appearance of impropriety, it wasn't illegal.).

The list of charges against Delaney grew. Other members of the department testified that Delaney had risked their safety during a sting operation involving undercover cops purchasing stolen goods. When those officers went to arrest the suspects in an early morning raid, they discovered that the press was already there, reporting live on the operation. One of Delaney's deputies had been wired to transmit the sounds of the arrest to reporters. The other cops were indignant that their safety would be compromised for publicity. Delaney admitted calling the reporters but said he didn't tell them where the raid would occur.

The verdict

In June 1981, the grand jury finally released its report. It found that DelBello had committed no offenses, although it took him to task for many deficiencies in both the structure of the merged police agency and the process used to create it, calling it "ill-conceived." DelBello was not at all surprised, admitting that the unusual conditions of Delaney's hire had created these vulnerabilities. He added he had never wanted an automatic five-year appointment for Delaney or anyone else. But that was the bargain he had to strike to create the new department. Everything that had happened, he argued, was why it was so important to bring all of Westchester County's police under civilian control.

The report's release was a wrist slap for DelBello but a job-ender for Delaney. He had been derelict in merging the departments. He had leveled false charges against DelBello. Even the "anonymous" letter claiming that DelBello and Carl Fulgenzi conspired to drop charges against the Bloomingdale's executive appeared to be a ruse, apparently written by one of Delaney's deputies to sully DelBello's reputation. This last offense alone amounted to fraud. It was exactly why DelBello believed that an unaccountable elected sheriff was such a fundamental danger. This single individual, armed with lies and innuendoes, could use the force of law to cripple an elected opponent politically and imprison him or her as well. This was more than dirty politics. It was a subversion of democracy of the kind we are witnessing today.

Delaney had one trump card left. Election season was well underway. He was in deep with Republican Joseph R. Pisani, the New Rochelle state legislator and future felon who would oppose DelBello in the county executive race. If Pisani got elected, Delaney knew his suspension would disappear with the defeated county executive. But as the election approached, the battle with the sheriff simply faded into the background. Despite a banner election year for Republicans, DelBello beat Pisani in a decisive victory. He even won Pisani's hometown of New Rochelle. The election was a testament to DelBello's success in reshaping county government and getting rid of corruption, which appealed to both sides of the political aisle.

With DelBello locked in for a third term, Delaney's bargaining power evaporated. Twenty-three serious charges remained. His own defense attorneys acknowledged in court that the accusation regarding Bloomingdale's executive was false. Given Pisani's loss, Republican legislators were quick to settle. Board of Legislators Chairman Ed Brady, concerned about an extended legal battle that had already cost the county $300,000, wanted an agreed-upon resignation. It would be one final devil's bargain for DelBello. Delaney got his retirement and a modest severance. All formal charges were dropped.

DelBello paid the price for his civilian-run police agency, but the inevitable fireworks were worth it. The creation of the new agency would never have been easy for any county executive. DelBello commented that no other administration could have gone through the legal challenges that his did and still come out with barely a bruise. To withstand the scrutiny of a public investigation, especially when instigated by Westchester's top cop, was something that almost no other politician could have survived. For true political professionals, such things are never easy. And like the professional he was, he would never have wanted it any other way.

CHAPTER 14

Enriching Westchester Life

"Three... Two... one...," the crowd chanted in unison. DelBello cut the ribbon. A cheer reverberated through the arboreal glade of the Bronx River Parkway at the opening of the first Bicycle Sunday. The cacophony of speeding cars had been silenced. The three-toned mourning of wood thrush and the quick clicks of cardinals flitting from tree to tree echoed from the dense, green canopy. The attendees, perched like songbirds on their bicycles, readied their balance and rode. DelBello and his wife Dee launched their two-seater without injury. One man heaved himself skyward into a tenuous, rocking balance on his "high-wheeler." "Don't call it a unicycle," he said with a smile.

It was a spectacularly sunny, warm day in June 1974. More than 1,000 elated people began their journey up a three-mile stretch of the Bronx River Parkway, from the edge of White Plains to the Kensico Dam in Valhalla. Cordoned off to cars, the bikers reveled in the first Bronx River Parkway "bike-in."

Many more car-free Sundays would come. (Today, "Bicycle Sundays" is open to in-line skaters, walkers, joggers and those on scooters from May through October, excluding holiday weekends, from Exit 4 at Scarsdale Road in Yonkers to Exit 22 at the Westchester County Center in White Plains, some thirteen miles.)

Never before in the county's history had a major road been closed to cars for the benefit of bikers and pedestrians. This had been one of DelBello's campaign promises. The event expressed his belief that planning and environmental protection should be participatory, just as government itself should be. He wanted open space and recreation in Westchester to be a tactile experience as well as a policy. For DelBello, it would also be a legacy.

Parkway to bikeway

The Bronx River Parkway Reservation was a magnificent, forested corridor built in the early part of the 20th century. The 807-acre elongated greenspace was Westchester's first county park, an adjunct to the roadway that snaked its length. Eponymously named, the parkway opened in 1925. It was the first "linear park" and the first parkway in the nation. It extended over nineteen miles through Westchester, from the New York City line in Yonkers north to the Kensico Dam Plaza in Valhalla. At the time of its construction, the new parkway concept was built with more than driving in mind. It was a forested escape to Westchester's undeveloped expanses. The scenery and fresh air were part of the driving "experience."

But as the population burgeoned in the second half of the century, the parkway became just another commuter link to

New York City. Though it was still beautiful at parkway speeds, DelBello believed it was important to reconnect people to the experience the parkway offered. On a bicycle cruising at six to eight miles per hour, he knew how much people would come to treasure it, even those harried daily commuters who had taken its environs for granted.

One of the people at the front of the biking convoy was Paul Feiner, Greenburgh's town supervisor since 1991 and the longest-serving elected executive in Westchester's history. But in 1973, he was a gangly teenager and biking fanatic who pestered county officials for more bicycle trails. Feiner met DelBello during a campaign rally when DelBello was first running for county executive. He petitioned DelBello to create more bicycle paths in Westchester to balance a growing road system devoted to cars. DelBello agreed. Feiner was impressed with the candidate's attentiveness and went to work on his campaign. When DelBello won, he put Feiner to work on developing a bike plan.

"Of all the public officials I have met, Al was a real doer," Feiner remembered. "He made Westchester visible. The county really changed because of him."

The parkway bike-in was the first step in a long-term plan for a Westchester bicycle network. Trails were proposed along the abandoned rights-of-way of the old New York and Putnam Railroad line, affectionately nicknamed "the Old Put," and the Croton Aqueduct. In a speech preceding the inaugural "Bicycle Sundays" event, DelBello said that he hoped to have as many as fifty miles of bikeways in a few years. Other north-south Westchester arterials for both road and rail were good candidates for bike trails, providing elegant park-like corridors. Although transportation bonds were stalled in the state Assembly, bikeway funds became available through the federal highway bill. DelBello jumped at the opportunity.

Conserving land – and history

Bikeways were but one part of a multi-pronged effort to enhance recreation and open space activities throughout the county. Westchester had grown rapidly. Development was outpacing open space protection. Fortunately, some large parcels of county land – generally those areas around reservoirs that supplied New York City and Westchester with drinking water – were already protected. But an estimated 50,000 undeveloped acres were at risk of rampant development. Those undeveloped lands protected water quality, local fisheries and habitat. Like a giant green sponge, these natural lands absorbed rainwater and filtered pollutants in the runoff while buffering residential and commercial areas from flooding.

In the 1970s, Westchester was a historic collection of forests, farms, parks, train lines, tight urban enclaves, residential subdivisions, shopping centers and highways. Unplanned growth was the landscape's greatest threat. Peter Eschweiler, DelBello's commissioner of planning, had served in the Michaelian administration to develop the county's master plan. That plan, six years in the making, was nearing completion. DelBello needed to get the plan out in front of the public and clarify his vision for the county. The recession would buy the county a brief respite from unplanned growth, but the pressures would soon return. He needed to enact the plan before the horses were once again out of the barn – or perhaps, more accurately, before the barn was torn down to make way for another residential subdivision.

The county's master plan targeted large land areas for protection while directing growth toward existing cities and towns. Those areas with existing development already had the infrastructure to service growth – things like water and sewer lines, roads and transit.

"The purpose (of the plan) is to encourage growth and development of our traditional centers of urban activity, such as the downtown shopping centers of our villages, towns and cities," DelBello noted, "and to discourage the 'urban sprawl' we have seen develop in other areas such as in New Jersey and on Long Island."

Good planning protected the county's budget, too. Sprawl was expensive. Widening roads and building sewer lines to retrofit unplanned growth was potentially a perpetual tax burden for citizens. To DelBello, growing where you already had the infrastructure was as economically sensible as it was ecologically sound.

By the middle of 1974, DelBello released the county's planning policy. Municipalities had control over zoning, and he had no intention of taking that away. The plan would not impinge on town land-use laws but rather use the county's investment power to encourage good local planning. The county's plan identified where water, sewer and transportation infrastructure would be built or improved – and where it would not. It was a clear message to local zoning boards that the county would not, in effect, "subsidize" growth outside of designated areas. DelBello had already (temporarily) halted construction of the Westchester Premier Theater in Tarrytown because the village's landfill operation was polluting Sheldon Brook. It was a clear message: The county wouldn't enable environmental problems. Planning and county investments would go hand in hand from that moment forward.

Investing in protected open space was the other side of the planning coin. Some argued that buying land for recreation and habitat was a high-cost luxury that competed with other spending priorities. DelBello knew the opposite was true. Protecting land and growing in the right places was a long-term fiscal benefit. Avoiding sprawl saved tremendous amounts of money on the construction of roads, water and sewer systems and other infrastructure. Times were tight, and costs were high. DelBello believed there was no more important priority for the county than land conservation.

He commissioned a county study that examined the effectiveness of acquiring land for watershed protection in contrast to water treatment. The study showed that this type of land planning would prevent ecological harm and avert expensive infrastructure in rapidly developing areas of the county. Westchester citizens were already seeing problems from overdevelopment. Repeated flooding in communities of older homes was occurring more frequently as upland areas were developed, causing more stormwater to rush downstream. The Bronx River Parkway was a testament to this. Located at the bottom of a river valley, its periodic flooding was worsened by continued development in the surrounding uplands.

For DelBello, the loss of open landscapes and rural land holdings to suburban development was something that threatened the county's identity. The town-and-country nature of Westchester was changing, due in part to the improving economic conditions that DelBello himself had fostered. The 18th-century Hyatt House in Scarsdale, on a large parcel of land, was facing demolition to build a suburban subdivision. (It is now the Cudner-Hyatt House Museum, a national landmark.) Lawyer Samuel J. Untermyer's Gilded Age estate in Yonkers had already been demolished because of the city's inattention to historic preservation – although its Greco-Persian landscape has been resurrected as the Untermyer Gardens Conservancy. The "feel" of Westchester was changing.

The county had the benefit of a number of wealthy patrons with large landholdings. Several of the nation's richest families – the Rockefellers and some of the Kennedys, among them – had made Westchester their home for generations. Some of these enormous estates had already become state reserves. Others, like the Rockefeller-owned Rockwood Hall, would be sold to the state as a new park – the Rockefeller State Park Preserve in Pleasantville. Westchester had part of New York City's water supply, as well as reservoirs of its own. This gave the county a head-start on open-space protection. But in the face of rapid development, the county's remaining open spaces were under threat.

DelBello with former Governor Averell Harriman and his wife Pamela Churchill Harriman at their estate in Katonah.

DelBello established a county goal of adding 5,000 acres in Westchester to the 13,000 already in permanent protection by the end of the century. Fortunately, there was almost $5 million in unspent capital appropriations for parks and open lands that remained unused when he took office. During an economic downturn, when real estate transactions were down and land prices were low due to high interest rates, this would be a lucky windfall. He would act quickly.

Saving Muscoot Farm

This funding source could also be used for capital improvements at existing parks. Muscoot Farm, the 777-acre preserve in Somers that the Michaelian administration had acquired, was the first park the DelBellos had visited after his election. It was a beautiful site, but only a remnant of the summer estate and dairy farm owned by the Hopkins family from 1880 to 1924. Fortunately, the house, outbuildings, and barns remained. Michaelian's administration had considered demolishing the structures to convert part of the site into an ice-skating rink.

DelBello believed Muscoot could be transformed back into an agricultural center with educational programs, tours and workshops for the county's citizens, especially children from more urban areas. He understood how important a public working farm was for teaching citizens not only about the history of agriculture, but also the economic and social value of farming in Westchester.

By late 1975, Muscoot Farm was up and running. DelBello budgeted for salaried professionals to operate the farm and create guided tours for school groups and senior citizens. Funded in part by foundation grants, the budget included an educational program about rural life, animal husbandry and arts and crafts. It introduced children to leather, textile, metalwork, ceramics and fine art. DelBello organized a press caravan to unveil the "living farm" to the public. It was a stunning, singular commitment to Westchester's past, present and future.

DelBello's vision for agriculture sometimes ran into shortages of money. He had – mistakenly – decided to end the county's support of 4-H clubs that, in turn, bolstered agricultural learning for children and to eliminate the County

Cooperative Extension Service. He got a quick lesson in their importance from the public. Residents from still-agricultural northern towns showed up en masse and pleaded for his reconsideration. People spoke about how the Extension Service kept them in business, and how 4-H is the kind of program "that holds on to kids." It was enough. DelBello put away his fiscal scythe.

"I have no problem with the board (of legislators) restoring the extension funds," he said. "I would encourage them to do so and would not veto it."

With young 4-H members at Muscoot Farm Park in Katonah.

Suburban recreation

Joseph M. Caverly, his new parks commissioner, had replaced Joseph Halper after a showdown between DelBello and the board of legislators had torpedoed his appointment. Caverly, who had grown up on a farm in Waverly, New York, had headed the San Francisco Recreation & Parks department. He was lured back east for the Westchester job. A true outdoorsman, Caverly liked to hike, camp and fish. Yet his background gave him an important insight into suburban issues such as swimming pools, city beaches and basketball courts, as well as remote natural parks.

DelBello directed him to work on smaller, urban recreation areas as well, including the pool at Glen Island Park in New Rochelle (the most visited park in Westchester) and the new ice-skating rink at Playland, the county's premier amusement park and beach area in Rye. He opened Cranberry Lake Park, a 146-acre nature preserve where people could fish and hike. This was important for the man from Yonkers. He knew city kids needed places they could go. Everybody had a recreational experience, urban or rural, that would connect them to where they lived. For DelBello, this was as important a defining characteristic of Westchester life as any.

DelBello believed that open space was not simply an amenity. Rather, it was part of the place that people called "home." He helped the county form a vision of its landscape. He reordered public spending around that vision by steering the county's infrastructure investments to those places where the growth had already occurred. And he steered open space funds to those undeveloped landscapes that needed protection – a "green infrastructure," so to speak, based on the same investment strategy as a sewer system or a highway. Once, when flying over the center of the county in a helicopter, he marveled at the intimate tapestry of lands below. He saw clusters of urban downtowns and traditional villages, tightly knit bedroom communities and commercial centers ringed with reservoirs, aqueducts, forests, fields and farms. The entire county lay before him, stretching from its northern heights to its southern border with the nation's most populous and dense city. It was a rich, diverse landscape of people and places, of city and country, of past and present – an undulating blanket of vibrant, green hills, swaddling history.

A heart for arts

There is an old saying in politics: Change is inevitable; survival is optional. As Westchester grew, it became a different place from its image as the sleepy bedroom community of New York City. Westchester was urbanizing and suburbanizing. Its demographics were changing. New people were moving in, and corporations were setting up shop. Many were relocating from New York City. They brought with them a desire for an arts and culture scene they had savored there, and that Westchester didn't have – at least not yet.

Despite being a chef's salad of city and country, a collection of locales with distinct personalities, Westchester had always maintained a shared identity that glued people together. County residents might tell one another what town they were from. But when speaking with people from out of the area, they would always say they were "from Westchester." Its evolving geographic persona set the stage for a new kind of culture. DelBello had always admired New York City for its vibrant cultural scene. Why shouldn't Westchester be its own cultural destination? he thought.

It was already becoming that. In 1967, Governor Nelson A. Rockefeller created the State University of New York (SUNY) College at Purchase, now Purchase College, primarily as an arts conservatory, with the public enticed to the campus by its developing Performing Arts Center and Neuberger Museum of Art – featuring the 20th-century collection of financier Roy R. Neuberger, a Rockefeller friend, and cutting-edge contemporary exhibits. A theater-in-the-round, the now-defunct Westchester Broadway Theatre, was planned for Elmsford in

Greenburgh. The 2,100-seat Loew's Theatre in New Rochelle – a Thomas W. Lamb-designed movie palace that had hosted major performers, such as coloratura soprano Beverly Sills – was under consideration as a mixed-use space. Another Lamb movie palace-turned-performing arts venue, The Capitol Theatre in Port Chester, became a premier home to rock 'n' roll acts (it recently celebrated its 95th anniversary). And though the intimate Emelin Theatre in Mamaroneck was struggling financially at the time of DelBello's tenure, it continued to host musical, dance and theater performances and rebounded financially over the years. These venues were an arts roadmap of Westchester's future.

Further enriching Westchester's cultural scene would necessitate a government partnership with corporations and private philanthropies. DelBello hoped working with a cross-section of nonprofits, corporations, educational institutions and local governments would create opportunities for new arts events and science fairs. Westchester, with its more open landscape, would be a cultural magnet for the entire southern New York region. Parks, corporate campuses and local colleges would provide superb settings for cultural happenings.

DelBello asked the Council for the Arts in Westchester (which became the Westchester Arts Council and now Arts-Westchester, the largest private cultural service nonprofit in New York State) to produce a comprehensive plan for cultural development. The Westchester Arts Council started very humbly in the kitchen of a DelBello friend, Janet Newlin, in Armonk. Dee remembers: "She prepared a delicious dinner for us. Polly Siwek, the arts leader for the county, was there, as well as other arts' supporters. Plans were made to launch an arts council with funds coming from the public and private sectors. It was the first time the arts were supported in both sectors." IBM was the first corporate benefactor, contributing $75,000.

"To my knowledge," the county executive said. "No suburban county government has put together an overall development plan for the arts and sciences that would guide both the public and private sectors." The council quickly established Westchester's Partners in the Arts, a collaborative of local artists funded by a federal grant. The "Arts in Public Places" program hired unemployed artists to create art projects throughout the county, including indoor and outdoor murals and sculptures. Even in a time of recession – or perhaps because of it – DelBello believed that art conveyed vision and hope. The council also provided a free or low-cost venue for people to enjoy the arts while on a tight budget.

Other "Arts in Public Places" venues included the Bridge Gallery on the enclosed bridge that connected the county courthouse in White Plains with the county office building. When the gallery opened in 1979, the arts committee had to seek out artists. Within a year, there was a waiting list for displays as artists sought out the Bridge Gallery as the desired venue. The county government also became a leader in supporting sculptures in public places, despite the cries from some naysayers who said the sculptures would be defaced. From the first day of sculpture installation to the present day, not one has been damaged or splattered with paint.

Corporate sponsors were generally quiet about the amount of their donations to arts projects – perhaps to avoid investors grumbling about expenses – but outspoken about their sponsorship. They wanted recognition. Their corporate names and logos often appeared in newspaper advertisements and on radio programs and stage banners. Prior to 1975, there had been no centralized way for corporations to contribute philanthropy to the arts. Emboldened by his commitment to businesses when Ed Michaelian first introduced him to the "Westchester 400," DelBello made them a part of his vision for the county.

As a result, the New York Philharmonic appeared at West-chester Community College in Valhalla, funded by large contributions from key Westchester corporations. One of the biggest public-private partnerships was "PepsiCo Summerfare," with PepsiCo – whose world headquarters in Purchase are the home of the magnificent Donald M. Kendall Sculpture Gardens – providing the financial support and across-the-street neighbor SUNY Purchase (Purchase College), the setting for the festival's run throughout the 1980s.

With composer Aaron Copland at his home in northern Westchester.

Meanwhile, square dancing, concerts and other events organized by the Department of Parks, Recreation and Conservation took place on county parkland. DelBello called all of it "an example of the creative spirit that has enabled Westchester County to develop as a major cultural center."

He also took the art message back to his roots in Yonkers. DelBello arranged for the city's board of education to rent the county-owned Wightman Estate for $1 per year to establish a "cultural arts center." The board would arrange concerts, plays, lectures, workshops and special student programs. Said its president, Joseph Sayegh, "It is a tremendous opportunity for the Yonkers school system and the county to work together on a project which will have far-reaching results for the future of Yonkers." Today the French Neo-Renaissance Wightman Mansion, part of Lenoir Preserve, is slated for a $5 million capital improvement project.

Public life on private shoulders

Many companies said that Westchester's rising level of corporate philanthropy was something they hadn't experienced on the same scale before, even in New York City. DelBello wanted more than just donations. He encouraged companies to participate directly in philanthropy for public transportation, housing and medical insurance. He helped broker a partnership between business and government to form the Westchester Opportunities Industrial Center. Port Chester, with a pocket of the county's highest unemployment rate, received job training and placement services that created 200 permanent jobs through the construction of a new office building, with profits reinvested in the community. Today the village is a multicultural home to restaurants and other eateries, and artisanal businesses.

Companies saw such partnerships as good for their reputations. DelBello saw them as the cornerstone of a better society – companies, government and citizens working together to solve problems and make the county healthier, richer and more inspiring.

It is difficult to fathom what Westchester would have looked like had it not been for DelBello's work. His was more than an issues-driven agenda. It was a mural of what a society of great and generous people should look like. It was a sculpture of life shaped by the hands of the citizens he inspired. It was a handcrafted landscape of vast open spaces – 18,000 acres in all, just as he had promised – carved out of an uncertain future. It was a portrait gallery of thriving urban streetscapes and city life.

DelBello's vision inspired millions of dollars in private funding and government grants to supplement county programs in arts, culture, open space and recreation. He received awards from the National Association of Counties for the Art in Public Places Program, the Senior Citizen Discount Program, the County Information Center, and several other organizations. Everyone wanted to be part of the county's rising star. DelBello was decades ahead of his political peers in his vision of Westchester as a full-fledged society rather than a residential adjunct to New York City. It was that vision that resisted the economic downturn of the mid-1970s, that sought to become rich in the face of scarcity, like a flower growing through a crack in the sidewalk. It was his "why not?" attitude, boldly articulated not despite the economic gloom but because of it, that defined his leadership better than anything else.

DelBello was never interested in his own glory, but rather in the posterity of his beloved county. Always painfully low-key and professorial, he once answered a reporter's question about opening the Bronx River Parkway to bicycles in a direct, unassuming way that reflected the reason for his eminent success:

"I think it's the right time for the right idea."

CHAPTER 15

Lockdown

The summer of 1981 was a particular sizzler across the New York metropolitan area. Children were eager to play outside on ball fields and in parks. Their parents sweltered in shorts and sundresses, while those that worked in corporate jobs were grateful for their air-conditioned offices.

A political pressure cooker was rapidly building steam as well. The Westchester County Jail, already overcrowded and under-cooled, had for years been the subject of attention from the press and a source of frustration in DelBello's office. The jail, located on the Grasslands Reservation in Valhalla, held inmates prior to their trials and before sentencing. The attached penitentiary housed prisoners for up to one year after their convictions. While most Westchester municipalities had their own local jails for short-term holdings, the county jail and penitentiary were the final stops for many of the county's inmates.

The jail had been built in the 1930s, a higher-capacity

replacement for Westchester's century-old prison facility. The prison was designed to house roughly 260 inmates. A separate women's correctional unit of roughly twenty inmates was opened on the bottom floor of the jail in 1967. The combined facilities were considered adequate at the time of their construction, but recent overcrowding and outdated internal security systems had become a problem. During the late 1970s, as many as 400 men were sometimes crammed into a jail built to house a little more than half that number. Prisoners were doubled up in small cells. Sanitation was inadequate, and recreation, library and vocational facilities were often unavailable because of security concerns from the overpopulation.

Pressure cooker

During DelBello's first year as county executive, he worried that overcrowding threatened the jail's safety. The newly-formed Westchester Association of Corrections and Probation Officers prepared a report for him critical of the administration at the county jail and penitentiary. In one incident, drugs were stolen from the penitentiary dispensary. Drug smuggling and use among prisoners were frequent, and one prisoner died from an overdose.

Poor supervision, lack of administrative support and staff turnover plagued the jails. Some inmates even claimed that they had a "better deal" than the corrections officers.

Most inside county government knew DelBello had inherited this problem. He took the report seriously, although he received immediate criticism from those who wrote it for not releasing it to the public, even though it contained confidential information. Drug abuse was a growing problem on city streets and in suburban enclaves alike. Violent crime associated with the drug trade was on the rise. More people were being arrested and incarcerated, and the nature of the prison population had changed. They were angrier, more dangerous, more defiant and, because of the drug trade, more numerous. DelBello, long a proponent of drug treatment programs such as Renaissance to rehabilitate addicts, had already taken several other more immediate actions, including hiring additional corrections officers to help with the problem of understaffing. He had also approved twenty-two additional jail cells in the 1980 budget and reluctantly supported the construction of seventy-five more. But he knew creating more jail cells wasn't the only solution.

One of his first and most important actions as county executive was in hiring Albert D. Gray Jr. as the new corrections commissioner. Gray had a solid, no-nonsense reputation and exemplary record. He had been a captain in the United States Marines. He had bachelor's and master's degrees from Columbia University and had served as a member of the New Jersey State Police. He became the superintendent of New Jersey's Trenton State Prison, home to some of the metro area's most notorious criminals.

When Gray joined the administration in 1974, he replaced Robert Wright, the longtime corrections commissioner, who had presided over the growing problems at the county correction facilities. Wright, only months from retirement, had been a competent public servant, but he didn't have the experience to handle the growing prison population and the more malevolent nature of the crimes that inmates had committed.

Only two weeks into his new job, Gray was quick to acknowledge some of the shortcomings that were being reported by corrections officers – understaffing in both the infirmary and kitchen, two places where thefts of material and equipment could easily result in physical harm or death; officers being pulled off their stations to accompany prisoners to court or the medical dispensary; shortages of corrections staff to conduct adequate searches for drugs and contraband; and an overall frustration among corrections officers that their concerns were falling on the deaf ears of supervisors.

The inmates complained as well. Overcrowding deprived inmates of recreational time. Facilities were unsanitary or inadequate. Proper medical care was lacking. Gray wanted inmates paid more adequately for in-prison work. He wanted more education and counseling programs to steer them away from drugs and crime when they were released. He also wanted an end to any abuse of prisoners. Prior to his arrival, there had been a number of suspected beatings and racial taunts inflicted by guards. No one was guiltless. Adequate staffing and oversight would be good for both inmates and corrections officers.

Gray immediately implemented new procedures for supervising inmates at the medical dispensary, where lax security posed the most significant problem. He acknowledged that much had been done on his watch to clean up some of the problems that had predated his command. Even the state Commission of Correction, while admitting to some ongoing problems, specifically cited Gray as having taken steps to improve the function of the facility, noting that the Westchester facility was run much better than other county jails. But overcrowding was still a challenge.

In some respects, that overcrowding was a measure of DelBello's success in clamping down on crime, something that voters had demanded. But that success was taxing an antiquated corrections infrastructure. DelBello had long suspected that a key problem was the bail process. The conditions of bail were too severe for low-level, nonviolent offenders, many of whom could have been released on their own recognizance or placed in less restrictive minimum-security halfway houses. The county jail simply did not have the capacity to house all of those whom the law had incarcerated, especially for pretrial holding.

By early 1981, DelBello had repeatedly appealed to Stephen Chinlund, chairman of the state's Commission of Correction in Albany, about prison overcrowding. In February, his administration sent a letter to the commission regarding the drastic shortage of space at the Westchester jail and the lack of temporary availability at other local jails and even state facilities, such as armories. DelBello enlisted the help of the board of legislators, passing a resolution to compel the state commission to comply with its own mandate to designate a location for detention when the county prisons run out of room. That appeal and subsequent appeals were completely ignored. DelBello threatened to initiate judicial proceedings.

He had, however, taken other steps. He formed a twenty-person "Task Force on Jail Overcrowding," made up of judges, commissioners, corrections staff, nonprofit directors and legal aid groups, which set an ambitious agenda to reduce the prison population quickly. Jail space wasn't the only concern. The group also addressed strategies to avoid recidivism as well as pretrial approaches to rehabilitation, such as alternative dispute resolution, drug counseling, psychiatric help, community service restitution and shoplifter-reform programs that would avoid incarceration altogether.

The task force participants were especially concerned with "intermittent sentencing" – weekend holdings of those arrested and indicted, which flooded the prison each Friday. Releasing many of them on their own recognizance would avoid the worst of overcrowding. The task force also agreed that bail was set too high for low-level offenders. One of Westchester's judges, Isaak Rubin, agreed to put together a meeting of county and local judges to reduce this somewhat arbitrary way of holding indicted people over the weekend. Treatment Alternatives to Street Crime (TASC), a nonprofit funded by the county's Department of Community Mental Health, had already recommended to Rubin the release of thirty-five inmates to take part in the program as an alternative to incarceration. DelBello called upon nonprofit and civic organizations to participate, so that crime prevention could be seen as a community challenge, not simply a law-enforcement matter.

DelBello had already arranged an ongoing program to hear from the prisoners about prison conditions. For weeks, a committee of inmates and prison staff had begun to examine facility problems from the inside. This was something that had never been tried before in Westchester. It made clear to the inmates that DelBello was serious about finding a solution to their plights. The staff of the committee reported to Warden Norwood Jackson. A former football player for the Cleveland Browns and an Airborne Ranger for the U.S. Army before moving into the corrections field, Jackson would eventually become correction commissioner himself. As warden, he reported the concerns of the committee to Commissioner Gray.

This initiative was timely, but not timely enough to reduce the jail's overcrowding in the sweltering summer heat. In late June, prisoners seeking to address some of the problems staged a peaceful demonstration at the jail. The protest was led by Khalil Mustafa, an inmate who had become an inside advocate for prison reform. But Mustafa, who was involved in the internal meetings, thought things weren't moving fast enough. He was worried about a riot. Ironically, he would be the one to light the fuse inadvertently.

Jailhouse rocked

Less than two weeks after the protest, Mustafa was suddenly transferred to Riker's Island in the East River between Queens and the Bronx. There was talk that he had been suggesting a violent prison revolt, though other prisoners with whom he had the discussion hadn't agreed to that. A listening device legally installed in the library had captured the conversation. Word of the transfer spread among the inmates. Around four thirty p.m. on July 10, during the early part of dinner time, roughly thirty inmates in the cafeteria began rioting, smashing dining hall furniture and yelling. The prison went on immediate lockdown. The corrections officers retreated, locking gates behind them and securing the riot within the cellblock area. But the damage was done. Cell doors were torn off their hinges and common areas were trashed. More than 300 men now had control of the prison.

DelBello was in his office on the ninth floor of the county office building in White Plains when the word came in. He was meeting with aides when his secretary put through the call. It was Commissioner Gray, who said, "The jail is rioting. We're on lockdown."

Stunned, DelBello was momentarily at a loss for words.

"Has anyone been hurt? Has anyone been taken hostage?" Gray could tell that DelBello was shaken.

"No, Al," Gray said. "Fortunately, all the corrections staff got out and locked the doors behind them. We got the administrative staff out. There's lots of noise, but I think so far this thing is basically without injuries." He paused. "We knew this was coming."

The county had already scored a small but significant victory in the riot: There were no hostages. That was not an accident. DelBello had worked for years to ensure an extensive training program that taught corrections officers exactly what to do in a prisoner uprising. When the riot began in the dining area, the officers immediately retreated and locked the doors and gates behind them. Then they evacuated the administrative offices. The prisoners were loose, but only within the same cellblocks they inhabited daily.

A number of the inmates knew that the county executive had been trying to improve prison conditions. DelBello had established a committee of prisoners and corrections officers to deal with the problem of overcrowding. He had been fighting for months to get more resources from the state. Word had certainly gotten around the prison that the county executive was at least trying to make things better. It may have saved lives.

Within the hour, the word "riot" was on every reporter's typewriter and on TV and radio. It was also on the lips of most Republican politicians, who were already eyeing a revolt of their own. The November election was just four months away. Given DelBello's contentious relationship with the former sheriff, Tom Delaney, the Republicans saw the riot as their golden opportunity. Paint DelBello as weak on crime and diffident on law enforcement, and they might triumph in November. Within hours, they were writing press releases and teaming up with the conservative-leaning police association.

"Where are you now?" DelBello asked Gray.

"I'm on my way back to Valhalla. I got word of this just as I stepped out of my kid's dental appointment. We set up a perimeter around the prison – lots of guards and police coming in from surrounding towns. I'll be there as soon as I can."

"Good. I'll call Coughlin in Albany and let him know we're on our way over there. He'll provide some backup," DelBello said with some relief, referring to Thomas Coughlin, the state corrections commissioner. "And Al," DelBello added, "let's make sure this thing goes as peacefully as possible. We know there are a few people who want to go in guns-a-blazin'. I don't want a repeat of Attica."

"I'm with you on that," Gray affirmed.

DelBello hung up. He asked his secretary to get Coughlin

on the phone right away to put the state's Corrections Emergency Response Team on alert. The CERT team was euphemistically referred to as "Orange Crush," a popular soft drink at the time. The disquieting nickname reflected the bright orange color emblazoned on the uniforms and their capabilities in riot suppression. The team stood ready with helmets, shotguns, mace and tear gas to quell any disturbance that might get out of hand. DelBello didn't think he would need them right away. But he might need them later, and he hoped their deployment would not end in bloodshed.

Ten years earlier, during the Attica prison riot, a number of corrections staff were taken hostage. Ultimately, the police and riot teams rushed the facility in a disastrous attempt to end the standoff. This action resulted in thirty-nine dead, including ten correction officers (an additional three inmates and a correction officer were killed at the beginning of the riot). Although there were no hostages in the Westchester riot – and the Westchester County Jail had less violent offenders than Attica – DelBello knew the wrong move could spark disaster.

Attica wasn't the only insurrection in the state's prison history. At the end of 1973, a series of small jail riots took place in Rockland County, across the Hudson River from Westchester. Although no one was gravely injured, a section of the facility was badly damaged. Clearly, jails throughout New York State had problems, and Westchester was no exception. It was a systemic issue that needed fixing. But right now, this was DelBello's problem. No corrections officers or prison staff were at risk. The inmates were contained. Anyone seeking to make political hay would do it regardless of the outcome. A peaceful resolution was his only priority.

Into the fray

DelBello and several aides arrived at the Valhalla prison complex shortly before five p.m. on what should have been a relaxing Friday evening. The area was swarming with police, EMTs, and reporters. About 230 heavily armed corrections officers and cops were gathered in a cordoned area outside the three-story prison. Many more were coming. All the municipalities in the county had provided aid in the form of police, fire, and medical assistance. The ninety-five-degree heat underscored the searing nature of the situation.

DelBello set up an emergency command center, run from an air-conditioned mobile trailer and powered by the same source that powered the lights for police operations and TV cameras. He arranged for aides to provide hourly updates to keep the press fully informed. Engaging the public would diffuse fear and act as a bulwark against the rumors and innuendoes that DelBello's political adversaries were already preparing. He and Gray used Gray's prison office as an internal command post.

Water and electricity were shut off at the start of the uprising to exert control over the prisoners. But DelBello knew that a forceful response could lead to violence. The prisoners were not organized. They were nervous, hot, flailing. He had to bring down the emotional temperature. The prison's listed capacity was 263 people, but there were 409 men inside awaiting trial or sentencing. Starting negotiations right away would calm things down.

DelBello's first step was to gain the trust of the inmates. He asked if Gray and Joseph M. Stancari, the assistant commissioner, would be willing to enter the facility. They agreed without hesitation. The two men, unarmed, had to ascend a ladder to the roof. Then they crawled through a heating duct to access the area where inmates had taken control. County staff, already in telephone contact with the inmates, announced the men were coming in.

Once inside, they were greeted by a small group of roughly twenty skeptical prisoners. But it had the right effect. They got the prisoners to agree to meet with the county executive. By that time, corrections officers were able to access one of the gates leading to the prison block. At roughly six p.m., DelBello entered the jail through the gates. He insisted that there be no corrections officers and no guns – just words. It was a risky move, but he believed that building trust was the key to ending the riot peacefully.

DelBello, Gray, and Stancari set up a conference table in the prison's gymnasium. They spent the next eight hours negotiating with the inmates and listening to complaints about overcrowding, restrictions on recreational and educational activities, and racial bias in the justice system. Although crimes were committed by a cross-section of society, the burden of imprisonment seemed to fall much more heavily on black and Latino men, who composed ninety percent of the prison population and faced mostly white juries – a situation that unfortunately has not changed much in this country. They objected to judges that casually set bail far beyond their financial means, often without regard to the severity of the crimes. They voiced concerns about periodic abuse from corrections officers. And it was hot, miserably hot. None of this was anything new to DelBello and his team, but they needed to hear it directly from the men themselves. And the men, in turn, needed to hear from him.

Around eleven p.m., a group of thirty men wielding broken pipes took over part of the women's facility (the women had been moved out). Apparently unaware of the ongoing negotiations between DelBello and their fellow inmates, they even broke through a wall in Gray's office, forcing a quick retreat by county correction and political staff. Yet by early Saturday morning, roughly two-thirds of the rioting prisoners had voluntarily returned to their cells. Negotiations with the remaining inmates continued, but no agreement had been reached. Exhausted after more than eight hours of discussion, DelBello, Gray and Stancari withdrew from the prison before dawn.

Not all the prisoners were cooperating, however. After a second outburst, DelBello called upon Coughlin to deploy Orange Crush. It was more of a display than a needed intervention – and it worked. The CERT team entered the prison yard, a wall of muscle, helmets and shotguns chanting in unison while marching in precise military syncopation. The parade elicited howls of derision and name-calling from many of the inmates. But it made the remaining rebels nervous. The inmates knew that the insurrection would end. The only choice they had to make was how it would end.

Perspiring through a short-sleeve shirt in the midday sun, DelBello reentered the prison's gymnasium, where he met with the inmates a second time. As they finalized the conditions of their surrender, the pipe-wielding marauders – who had become an irritation throughout the entire insurrection – broke through a concrete wall outside the gymnasium and tried to enter through the gym doors.

A novel security team was at the ready – a band of volunteer firefighters armed with a hose. A blast of water greeted the assailants, forcing them back. It was a successful and almost comical alternative to tear gas, billy clubs, and guns. The insurrectionists ran from the gymnasium doors. The talks continued.

Richard Ali Lindsay – a man whose last name reminded DelBello of the former mayor of New York City – was the inmates' lead negotiator. Bright and serious, Lindsay accepted a list of compromises. It wasn't everything the inmates wanted, but it was a lot more than they had a day earlier. In a press conference on the gym's basketball court, DelBello and Lindsay announced their terms before a microphone, with members of the press in attendance. A review of all inmate requests for bail reduction would begin Monday morning. Administrative Judge Joseph Gagliardi would have face-to-face discussions with the inmates concerning their grievances. District Attorney Carl Vergari would meet with the inmates in a subsequent listening session. Inmate representatives would meet monthly with DelBello. Perhaps most importantly, there would be no physical or legal reprisals against any inmate. At the conclusion of the negotiations, Lindsay shook DelBello's hand. "We will allow ourselves to be locked in tonight," he said.

The riot was over without a single shot fired. All the inmates, including Lindsay and his fellow negotiators – lined up in the prison yard to accept orders from the CERT team. Within minutes, the inmates were stripped naked and searched. All the cells were scoured, and any homemade weapons or contraband were removed. Most of the cell doors were damaged and unsecured, but the inmates agreed to reside there for the night.

Yet on Sunday, the corrections officers walked off the job. Although the riot had essentially ended, they felt they weren't being treated fairly and that their safety had been compromised – even though they had spent the duration of the uprising in a secure area away from the prison melee. As a result, nurses who had shown up to work to assist with any injuries that might have occurred were forced to abandon their own posts. Once again, it seemed that police and corrections officers were lined up against DelBello, despite his having ended the riot peacefully.

During the next few weeks, the jail was gradually repaired. Inmates and corrections officers returned to their normal activities. The event was not without repercussions for both DelBello and the officers. There were serious charges of vengeful punishment by the CERT team, physical mistreatment, denial of showers, with prisoners being tightly handcuffed, pushed around naked, threatened and humiliated. The event could have been DelBello's political downfall. The fallout from the riot would raise every political hackle the Republicans could muster. And it would be led by his November challenger in the county executive election, State Senator Joseph Pisani.

The Monday-morning rebellion

The first real "shots" of the riot were fired Monday morning. Issuing an absurdly late press release, the Tri-County Federation of Police Inc. began blasting away at the two Als, DelBello and Gray. They viewed DelBello's cool strategy as a missed opportunity to use brute force. They asserted that the CERT team should have been deployed Friday night rather than using orderly military precision that peacefully ended the insurrection by Sunday. It was like yelling "fire" after the firefighters had already extinguished the blaze.

Pisani, the Republican Party's primary pick for county executive, sent DelBello a letter – widely circulated to the public – ripping him for everything that had happened. The letter failed to mention that not a single weapon had been deployed (except for a firehose) and that the riot had ended peacefully with the ascent of the inmates.

More press release than correspondence, the letter opined:

"The destructive, humiliating, and financially disastrous events of last weekend at the County Jail are without precedent in the history of Westchester County. You and your subordinates have sent a clear message to the violent underworld that physical defiance, rioting, vandalism, and open rebellion will be rewarded by high-level negotiations and concessions." The remainder of the letter was full of accusations, most of them patently false, that an uprising wasn't anticipated (DelBello had warned about it for months), that they had done nothing to prevent it or that the administration failed to "contain and suppress" the uprising.

But DelBello had letters of his own – all the letters he had sent to the state Commission of Correction months earlier, demanding help with overcrowding. He reminded voters of the Jail Overcrowding Task Force he had established weeks before the riot, the work he had done with state judges on pretrial holding reform, cooperating with local nonprofits on alternatives to jail, and proposing counseling programs to reduce recidivism. Most important, he had indeed contained and suppressed the uprising without violence, ending it within thirty-six hours.

Later that week, Pisani held a press conference in which he stated that he would have retaken the facility "by force with gas" and weapons. He claimed officers were attacked and held in "armlocks and headlocks," despite no evidence of such assaults. Gray, responding in back-to-back press conferences, retorted that such action would have led "to a mass graveyard."

But DelBello was already a step ahead of his challenger. By the time Pisani's press conference started, some of the revised bail conditions that had been peacefully negotiated during the riot were already taking effect. Of eighty-seven cases reviewed, four inmates were released on their own recognizance, including one who had originally been given a bail of $500 for petty larceny weeks earlier and another jailed with a hefty bail for fourth-degree mischief and harassment. It was clear that prison overcrowding was due, at least in part, to unnecessary pretrial holding procedures.

Re-elect
County Executive
Del Bello.
He's got the courage
to do what's right.

DelBello campaigning for re-election as county executive.

Several county legislators tried to feed on Pisani's argument. Egged on by the unprepared, careless testimony of one of the prison system's associate wardens, Ed Brady and Joseph William Christiana Sr., Republicans from Thornwood and Mount Vernon, respectively, called for Gray's resignation. Get rid of one "Al," they thought, and the other might fall. Gray, however, wasn't going to budge. Diane A. Keane, a southern county Republican, accused Gray of having done no riot-control training and not having chemical agents (such as tear gas) for such emergencies. But Gray provided a memo detailing the extensive emergency training his department had undertaken during the previous four years.

Keane headed the temporary Committee on Corrections, created by DelBello's former Yonkers City Council colleague and now Board of Legislators member Andy O'Rourke. The committee's purpose was to find solutions to the problem of overcrowding in the county jail. It became a fishing expedition to net DelBello in advance of November's election. A trail of accusatory letters and condescending requests for county administrative staff to appear before the board seemed to counter the committee's purpose. DelBello noted in response to Keane that he had specifically briefed the board of legislators on the first day of the riot and had arranged a tour of the facility for the legislators afterward. He added that dealing promptly with jail problems to prevent another uprising was paramount and should be done without regard to politics. He still offered his cooperation but warned her he wouldn't tolerate a witch hunt.

A report on the riot from the state Commission of Correction – the same agency that had been so unhelpful during the months leading up to the riot – was filled with a number of errors. Perhaps most frustrating, the report was created without interviewing any county staff, including DelBello and Gray. DelBello, in a letter to the state commissioner, expressed in writing his objection to these mistakes. But then he switched gears – as he always did – addressing each item in the commission's report, correcting errors, stating where progress had been made, promising frequent updates and welcoming further responses. He requested that the state commission interview him and all senior corrections staff. He offered his help in any way he could. It was DelBello's go-to strategy – always be focused and forward-looking, even when frustrated.

Justice no longer delayed

In the coming months, DelBello oversaw much-improved systems for bail, sentencing and alternatives to incarceration. Prison crowding was on the decline. New equipment and facilities replaced those destroyed in the riot, and corrections officers were given better training. Prisoners met regularly to voice complaints and provide input. Once again, Westchester County became a model for the rest of the state. Other county jails, correction officials and state agencies rushed to catch up. DelBello had turned a crisis on its ear, furthering Westchester's preeminence as a national leader in public policy.

The Republican-led State Senate cobbled together its own partisan report. A State Senate minority report, submitted by Democrat Jeremy Weinstein, was much more realistic. It highlighted the problems county officials had faced in finding alternative prison sites to ease overcrowding and praised the county for its innovative programs to prevent pretrial incarceration and reduce recidivism.

Perhaps no public statement made as clear the success of DelBello's response to the riot as a letter he received from the Institute of Judicial Administration. Robert B. McKay, the institute's director, had been directly involved with the New York State Special Commission on Attica a decade earlier. He acknowledged the desperate situation New York and many other states faced with prison overcrowding. But he also highlighted what he saw in DelBello as an exceedingly rare and valued attribute:

"Although the uprising and takeover of the county jail constituted grave threats to the security of the institution and to the safety of correction officers and inmates, it is truly remarkable that the matter was resolved without physical injury to any of the participants. When the institution was completely under the control of the inmates, there must have been a very real temptation to use force to regain control. In my judgment, you and your colleagues who have principal responsibility for the county jail exercised admirable restraint in rejecting the use of force. It was an act of great courage for Commissioner Gray and Associate Warden Stancari to enter the jail immediately after the takeover, unarmed except with the power of persuasion. When you negotiated with the inmates inside the institution on the following day, that, too, was brave. I commend all three of you for achieving a peaceful resolution of the uprising without any diminution in your authority while gaining new credibility with the inmates."

The Republicans had made a perilous political mistake. They thought the prison riot would be the crystalizing issue for the 1981 election. It wasn't. Ironically, another law enforcement issue – the grand jury hearings examining the corrupt former Republican sheriff, Tom Delaney – may have acted as a counterweight to Pisani's accusations about DelBello's culpability in the riot.

But the more likely case was that people simply weren't concerned. Crime was down more than sixteen percent in six months. The economy was booming. Arts and culture, youth programs, public transportation and environmental protection were roaring ahead. The Westchester Medical Center was heading toward financial independence. The new waste-to-energy plant would soon begin construction, relieving taxpayers of tens of millions of dollars in waste remediation costs. Westchester was a much better place to live. And DelBello had made it so.

Three months later, he soundly defeated Pisani, ushering in his third – and final – term as Westchester County executive.

CHAPTER 16

Citizen DelBello

DelBello's transition from politics to the private sector after he resigned as lieutenant governor on February 1, 1985, may have seemed seamless, but it was still a difficult adjustment. The transition was made easier by his first private-sector job as president and CEO of Signal Environmental Systems Inc., the same company that owned Westchester's new trash-to-energy plant. The plant was one of the legacy changes he had brought to the county, laboring for close to a decade to create the first-in-the-nation regional facility of its kind. The project had saved taxpayers tens of millions of dollars in disposal costs and years of litigation over the bursting Croton Point Landfill. Signal planned to take the energy-producing technology to many other places, and it knew DelBello's political skills would help them do it.

Critics charged conflict of interest. But DelBello said, "The reason I got into this business was because I pioneered the privatization of public services in Westchester County." He noted that when a government contracts with a private vendor, the company designs, builds, owns and operates the plant, relieving the government of management and unexpected costs. He believed this idea of a "public-private partnership" was the future of government.

He had done this before. As county executive, he had consolidated a collection of private transportation companies to create a unified county bus service. He had negotiated between private plane companies and residents to make the Westchester County Airport a regional air hub. And he had birthed the Westchester Medical Center, arguably his greatest, most lasting county legacy, with a large county capital investment, ultimately handing it off to the private sector once it had stabilized. DelBello had long been convinced that private enterprises, working in partnership with local, state and federal government, could provide vital services to the public at a much lower cost. Federal mandates were increasing while federal funding was decreasing. "The question is not whether to privatize," he said, "but how...."

DelBello had a knack for interlacing issues and solving multiple problems at once. After the waste-to-energy plant opened, the closed Croton Point Landfill was converted into the 500-acre Croton Point Park with magnificent views of the now-cleaner Hudson River, exactly as he had planned before leaving the county for the lieutenant governor's office. He turned the Bronx River Parkway into a Sunday bicycle path, spurring demand for many more full-time bikeways. His kaleidoscopic grasp of complex problems was exceeded only by the innovative, interdisciplinary solutions he offered. His "why not?" ethic became the catalyst that made Westchester one of the most successful, financially stable counties in the nation. DelBello's accomplishments as county executive mattered greatly, but he also began so many initiatives and plans that continued far beyond his time in the county executive's suite, leaving an enduring legacy for Westchester long after his departure.

Fighting for youth

As a citizen and leader, DelBello remained committed to local and state political issues. He became the president of the National Council on Teenage Suicide, which he had founded in 1983 while still serving as lieutenant governor. And he was named chairman of the capital fund drive for Odyssey House, a residential center for youth troubled by drug and alcohol abuse in Hampton, New Hampshire, where Signal's main office was located.

"As mayor of Yonkers, I was involved in the Renaissance program in the 1970s, which is similar to the program at Odyssey House," he said. "When the people at Odyssey House asked me to serve, I was a little surprised since I had just come to New Hampshire. But I am pleased to do what I can."

Conserving the land

From 1987 to 1992, he ran his own environmental consulting firm. So, it was no surprise that he would join the Westchester Land Trust board in 1988, serving as its chairman from 1994 to 1999. During that time, "the land trust completed twelve preservation projects protecting 225 acres, including a conservation easement over 137 acres of Bedford's historic Coker Farm," The Journal News' Keith Eddings wrote in a May 5, 2008 article. "DelBello also takes credit for refocusing the trust's work on land preservation, steering it away from the community gardens and education programs that he said were diversions."

But as Eddings observed, by this time, DelBello was also "the marquee partner in Westchester's most prominent land-use law firm," the White Plains-based DelBello Donnellan Weingarten Wise & Wiederkehr LLP, whose clients including former U.S. President Donald J. Trump and Louis R. Cappelli were some of the heaviest hitters in the region's development..

Again, the charge of conflict of interest reared its head. But DelBello, who told Eddings he maintained "a Chinese wall" between his land trust duties and law work, had always seen the importance of linking development and open space protection, not only to preserve nature but also to enhance the attractiveness and the value of new development. Having issued Westchester's first master plan shortly after becoming county executive, he emphasized the importance of linking development to land preservation.

As to all things, he brought a personal touch, remembered John R. Nolon, distinguished professor of law emeritus at the Elisabeth Haub School of Law at Pace University and creator of the school's Land Use Law Center. Nolon, who was the deputy director of the department of development in Yonkers, recalled meeting DelBello in 1971 as he was walking to work. DelBello was campaigning for his second term as mayor. Never was a single handshake and greeting better remembered:

"When I shook his hand, it was warm, and the handshake lingered. He didn't quickly pull it away, nor was the shake forceful and overbearing. I immediately thought he was a likable guy, genuine, not stuck on himself and always interested in doing what was in the public interest."

It was a first impression that would last for decades. Nolon admired DelBello for his visionary land planning. He remembered his work finalizing Westchester's master plan and his commitment to making land use a lynchpin of public policy – particularly affordable housing, something both men had advocated years earlier in Yonkers. Nolon said that DelBello went after federal Community Development Block Grant funding as county executive, greatly expanding Westchester's affordable housing program. He praised DelBello's pivotal service on the board of the Westchester Land Trust, running meetings with professionalism and humor.

"Al felt that his role was not about manipulation or power struggles, but people," Nolon added. "All people involved had different perspectives on issues, and those perspectives needed to be respected."

Minding the county's business

William M. Mooney Jr. agreed. The director of community and institutional relationships at Simone Healthcare Development and the former president and CEO of the Westchester County Association, an organization serving a range of civic and economic goals that DelBello also chaired, always considered himself more a Republican than a Democrat. Yet he adored DelBello, and compared him to Presidents Ronald Reagan and Bill Clinton, noting his ability to get things done by working across the aisle.

"He was the most bipartisan guy I ever met in my life," Mooney remembered. "He always did things for the public good."

The two men got to know each other when DelBello became chairman emeritus of the WCA in 2006. He noted, in particular, DelBello's ability to speak extemporaneously on a range of issues citizens cared about, displaying a remarkable breadth of in-the-pocket knowledge. "He fearlessly stood up for what he believed was right," Mooney said.

This was particularly true of his passion for workforce development and affordable housing as well as environmental protection and health care. At first glance, these issues might not seem the centerpiece of business, but DelBello saw them as essential for attracting and sustaining businesses and institutions and the people who worked for them. He knew that economic, environmental and social sustainability undergirded a healthy society.

Yet he understood how business worked – sometimes more for profit than community well-being. Mooney recounted how the Westchester Medical Center and other hospitals were getting squeezed by health insurance companies. In the mid-2000s, they pressured the hospitals through a series of retroactive audits to recover some of the payments they had previously made. The "inefficiencies" for which they wanted partial reimbursement went back as far as five years, when procedures in the rapidly evolving medical field were different. The big health care companies used the recovered money for marketing and advertising while practically negotiating hospitals out of business. DelBello thought it a bit of a scam.

So, he led the WCA in a campaign to challenge the reimbursement audits. The group conducted an eight-month study that addressed a number of "market conduct" issues – polite words for gouging – that detailed the greedy practices of the health companies. The study got the attention of other counties and even the state legislature. The health care companies backed down. Future audits were limited to the previous year only, where cost overruns could be examined in the context of current medical practices.

Visionary, leader, family man

Not everyone was as admiring as Mooney. As lieutenant governor in the administration of Mario Cuomo, with whom he had a thorny relationship, DelBello had remained committed to the job. Friends and colleagues had advised him to quit before the inauguration, but he refused. He had made a promise to voters. It was far more important than his political success. It was the right choice for posterity. But it was a bruising experience, one that would echo after his death on May 15, 2015.

At the 2018 funeral of former DelBello aide Andrew Zambelli Jr., who stayed on to work for Cuomo after DelBello departed state government, then-Governor Andrew Cuomo delivered a rambling eulogy highlighting the difficult relationship between his father and DelBello. He noted that "... my father had been offended by things DelBello had said during the campaign, and he refused to have any deep, meaningful conversation with the new lieutenant governor. The deep, meaningful conversation included terms such as, 'Hello, how are you?'" Andrew Cuomo said, trying to elicit an uncomfortable laugh. "The work to repair the governor and lieutenant governor's relationship went on for months," he added.

Some things, once lost, cannot be regained. In 1994, DelBello tried to reenter politics with a run for the State Senate. But the Republican tide was against him. He lost to Vincent Leibell III, a New York State Assemblyman from Putnam County who would later be convicted on federal corruption charges.

DelBello's defeat, especially after so many years out of the game, was not completely unexpected. "I just needed to get it out of my system," DelBello said. Office holding may no longer have been in the cards for him, but he continued supporting

Democratic politicians, including Hillary Clinton, former U.S. secretary of state and the first woman to win the presidential nomination from a major political party, former New York State Governor Eliot Spitzer and Carl McCall, his one-time lieutenant governor opponent and good friend. Had the cards fallen differently, DelBello might have risen to the governorship and then the national political scene. His innovation, business sense and flexible, pragmatic leadership might have made the Democratic Party and America itself very different.

With President Bill Clinton.

Mooney remembered DelBello not only as a leader but also as a man, one who worked with his son, Damon, to restore a 1969 Jaguar XKE; who would do his own construction, often driving a bulldozer and other heavy equipment around his elegant northern Westchester property, which he and his equally animal-loving wife Dee had filled with alpacas, chickens, peacocks and dogs – especially their beloved West Highland Terriers. "We really lost a great resident of Westchester and a great father and husband, too," Mooney added.

Dee DelBello remembers her husband's love of animals as well. She noted, "From his early childhood, Al loved animals, from crawly insects to two-legged feathery birds to four-legged dogs, cats, even raccoons. He rescued them when they were injured, restored them to good health and set them free." She remembers him rescuing one of the family's first dogs, a Westie named Sollo, after it had fled the property.

"Al ran after it for miles until he caught him in a muddy pond. This sensitive, caring side of a very private man came through as a public man when he created offices and services for the poor, the impaired, for women and for consumers who may have suffered from unfair business practices." The rescued Westie remained the family pet for fourteen years.

Dee also recalls a feral cat Al had discovered in Yonkers. When he came across it during the workday and tried to pet it, it bit him! But he knew the cat needed help. He came back and managed to coax the cat into a cage, then donated it to a friend who took in strays. The cat went from the gritty streets of Yonkers to a luxurious home in northern Westchester. He had a deep and abiding concern and compassion for all living things that went beyond his allegiance to people. It was part of his obligation to a society that had given him much.

He was "a genuine Renaissance man and an omnipresent figure in the county," said Geoff Thompson, part of the senior management team at the Briarcliff Manor, New York-based public relations firm of Thompson and Bender who possessed an encyclopedic knowledge of all things Westchester. And the county remembered that in 2016, renaming Muscoot Farm after him, a legacy county property in which DelBello had played an integral role in its rebirth as an interactive farm.

What strikes everyone as remarkable is that this man of

grace and decency might have just as easily slipped from public prominence had he not succeeded in politics. But his success wasn't simply luck. He was a visionary – determined and daring. He was willing to take political risks by working outside of party boundaries. He believed, obsessively, that life could be better if citizens were brought into the political fold, for they would see their destiny as inextricably tied to everyone else's. A complex person, he synthesized equally complex solutions from the fragments of neverending challenges that came his way, as if sewing a telltale tapestry of history and hope from the intimate swatches of Westchester's intricate, beautiful life.

BIBLIOGRAPHY

Editor's Note

Williams, Lena, "A Look Back at DelBello's 20 Years in Politics," *The New York Times*, Jan. 13, 1985.

John Jordan's obituary of Alfred B. DelBello, *Real Estate In-Depth*, June 25, 2015.

Daniel E. Slotnik's obituary of Alfred B. DelBello, *The New York Times*, May 17, 2015.

CHAPTER ONE: Flyover Country

Frank Nardozzi's interview with Alfred B. DelBello.

Oreskes, Michael, "DelBello's 'Shotgun Wedding' With Cuomo is Working Out," The New York Times, Sept. 5, 1984.

CHAPTER TWO: When Mario 'Met' Al

Frank Nardozzi's interview with Alfred B. DelBello.

Interview with Roger Biaggi.

"New York's Sanguine Politics," *The New York Times*, June 17, 1978.

"The Man Who Loved New York," *Times Union*, Aug. 8, 2011.

"Cuomo Beats Koch In Democratic Primary; Leherman, Moynihan and Mrs. Sullivan Win," *The New York Times*, Sept. 24, 1982.

"Several Assess Chance to Win Party Primary," *The New York Times*, Jan. 16, 1982.

"How Koch is Doin' in Editorials Across the State," *The New York Times*, March 1, 1982.

"Koch Holds 11 Pt. Lead in Gov Race," *New York Post*, Sept. 13, 1982.

Oreskes, Michael, "DelBello's 'Shotgun Wedding' With Cuomo is Working Out," *The New York Times*, Sept. 5, 1984.

"DelBello Drops His Pearl Harbor Day Bomb," *Sunday Freeman*, Dec. 23, 1984.

CHAPTER THREE: A Marriage of Inconvenience

Wolf, Richard, "DelBello Bids Farewell With No Regrets," *The Journal News*, Jan. 30, 1985.

Haberman, Clyde, "The Lessons of Attica: 25 Years Later," *The New York Times*, Sept. 10, 1996.

Interview with David Tooley, special assistant to Al DelBello.

Lynn, Frank, "A Rivalry in the Making: Miss Shaffer vs. DelBello," Sept. 7, 1983.

"Panel to Combat Suicide by Youths," *The New York Times*, Sept. 30, 1984.

"Meeting in Westchester Looks at Youth Suicides," *The New York Times*, Oct. 26, 1984.

"Readers Vote Teen Suicides the Top News Story of 1984," Jan. 1, 1985.

"Needed: A U.S. Commission on Teenage Suicide," *The New York Times*, Sept. 12, 1984.

DelBello, Lt. Gov. Alfred B., Economic Development Report to the Governor, 1984.

Whitehouse, Franklin, "Cuomo Sets Up Committee to Review Yonkers Finances," *The New York Times*, Jan. 7, 1984.

"DelBello Drops His Pearl Harbor Day Bomb," *Sunday Freeman*, Dec. 23, 1984

"DelBello to Visit Asia for 'Trade Mission'" *The New York Times*, April 29, 1983

Interview with Alfred B. DelBello.

"Decision Has Experts Wondering," *The Reporter Dispatch*, Dec. 8, 1984.

CHAPTER FOUR: Beginnings, or 'What Have You Got to Lose?'

Frank Nardozzi's interview with Alfred B. DelBello.

CHAPTER FIVE: The Clean-Up Hitter

Interview with Dee DelBello.

https://obits.lohud.com/us/obituaries/lohud/name/james-o-rourke-obituary?pid=149417741

Report of the State Investigation Committee, 1970.

Editorial, "Our Choice Again: Mayor O'Rourke; But the Big Thing is To Vote," *The Herald Statesman*, Nov. 3, 1969.

Hurley, Denis M., "DelBello Lashes Republicans for Rejecting City Budget," *The Herald Statesman*, Dec. 27, 1969.

Andover, James, "Scher Meets Council; Huddles with Manager," *The Herald Statesman*, January 16, 1970.

Peterson, Iver, "Big Six Mayors Tour Yonkers and Find Common Problems," *The New York Times*, Jan. 30, 1970.

Holcomb, Charles R., "Big Six Mayors Press for Aid," *The Herald Statesman*, Jan. 13, 1971.

"Governor Tell Big 6 Mayors; Chances for Aid are Very Small," *The Herald Statesman*, Dec. 17, 1970.

"Revenue Sharing Backed," *The Herald Statesman*, Jan. 25, 1971.

Tritton, Jennie, "Police, City Together on New 2-Year Pact," *The Herald Statesman*, May 26, 1972.

"Intruder Enters Longfellow as Mayor Tours School," *The Herald Statesman*, Jan. 8, 1971.

Hurley, Denis M., "When You're Mayor, You're Busy," *The Herald Statesman*, Feb. 10, 1971

"Mayor to Longfellow Students: City Will Check, Repair School," *The Herald Statesman*, Jan. 13, 1971.

Martin, Neil S., "Yonkers Getting More U.S. Funds," *The Herald Statesman*, March, 1971.

"Mayor Shares Award for interracial Justice," *The Herald Statesman*, Nov.12, 1970

"Rent-A-Kid Idea Caching On," *The Herald Statesman*, August 14, 1971.

"CAMP Begins as HEY Ends," *The Herald Statesman*, Sept. 3, 1970

Miller, Jacqueline, "CAP Director Speaks on Her 'New Thrust'," *The Herald Statesman*, March 16, 1971.

Tritten, Jennie, "City Youth Service Agency Wins 13-0 Council Approval," *The Herald Statesman*, March 24, 1971.

"Renaissance Program to Get 'Sing Out' Aid," *The Herald Statesman*, June 3, 1970.

"Welfare Paid the Bill," *The Herald Statesman*, Jan. 14, 1971

"DelBello Requests Housing Meeting," *The Herald Statesman*, Aug. 12, 1971

Martin, Neil S., "Scher Seeks Aid for City Renewal," *The Herald Statesman*, Feb. 1, 1971

Alfred B. DelBello mayoral campaign literature, "In Its First Term, the DelBello Administration...."

"Rent Office in City Hall Completed," *The Herald Statesman*, Nov. 12, 1970.

"DelBello to Argue for Tenants' Union," Daily News, Oct. 28, 1971.

Tritten, Jennie, "Candidates Trade Blows Over MHA Tenant Strike," *The Herald Statesman*, July 22, 1971.

"Tenants Council Backs Martinelli," *The Herald Statesman*, Oct. 26, 1971.

Martin, Neil S., "Relocation Office Opens Along Nepperhan Route," *The Herald Statesman*, May 5, 1971.

"City Council Endorses Transportation Bond," *The Herald Statesman*, Oct. 27, 1971.

"Waterways Orchestra Climaxes Festival," *The Herald Statesman*, Aug. 7, 1972.

"Waterfront Development Issue Rages," *The Herald Statesman*, Oct. 22, 1971.

"Mayor DelBello to Host Radio Program," *Yonkers Record*, April 30, 1970.

CHAPTER SIX: Garbage, Guns and Guts

Hoffman, Milton, "Grand Jury Probers Cite Mismanagement," *The Herald Statesman*, July 7, 1970.

Moran, Nancy, "Yonkers Is Bedroom and Office for Mafia Chiefs," *The New York Times*, Feb. 25, 1970.

Andover, James, "Scher Meets Council; Huddles with Manager," *The Herald Statesman*, January 16, 1970.

Tritten, Jennie, "Candidates Trade Blows Over MHA Tenant Strike," *The Herald Statesman*, July 22, 1971.

"Tenants Council Backs Martinelli," *The Herald Statesman*, Oct. 26, 1971.

"Martinelli is Slum Breeder," *Yonkers Record*, Sept. 30, 1971.

CHAPTER SEVEN: Days of the Jackals

Martin, Neil S., "City Manager Scher Resigns," *The Herald Statesman*, Jan. 12, 1972.

"Rising Costs Call for New Thinking," *The Herald Statesman*, Sept. 14, 1971.

Donovan, Dan, "Strikers Mass at City Hall," *The Herald Statesman*, January 7, 1972.

Greenhouse, Linda, "Teacher Walkout Ends in Yonkers," *The New York Times*, Jan. 14, 1972.

"Scher Confidence Vote Set Tonight," *The Herald Statesman*, Jan.13, 1972.

Interview with Alfred B. DelBello.

"Mayor: No More 'Plums'," *The Herald Statesman*, Jan. 17, 1972.

Randazzo, John. "Mayor Calls on Council to Return Scher," *The Daily Argus*, Jan. 13, 1972.

"CM Confidence Vote Draws Mayor's Ire," *The Record of Yonkers*, Jan. 13, 1972

"Scher Vote 10-2; Won't Quit City," *The Herald Statesman*, Jan. 13, 1972.

"Scher Confidence Vote Set Tonight," *The Herald Statesman*, Jan. 13, 1972.

"Police Job Action Set for Midnight," *The Herald Statesman*, Feb. 16, 1972.

Tritten, Jennie, "Police, City Together on New 2-Year Pact," *The Herald Statesman*, May 26, 1972.

"State Aid Needed to Avert Crisis, Big 6 Mayors Say," *The New York Times*, Feb. 18, 1971.

"Mayor Declares 'Revenue-Sharing Day'," *The Herald Statesman*, Feb. 20, 1971.

"DelBello Says City Will Get Less Than Promised," *The Herald Statesman*, Jan. 23, 1971.

Narvaez, "Six Mayors Warn of 'Mass Layoffs'," *The New York Times*, March 31, 1971.

"$4.2 Million Freshens Budget," *The Herald Statesman*, April 4, 1971.

"Yonkers Getting More U.S. Funds," *The Herald Statesman*, March, 1971.

"Revenue Sharing Passed by House," *The New York Times*, Oct. 13, 1972.

Farrell, William E. "State Budget $8.8-Billion; Spending Up $933-Million, But No Tax Rise is Sought," *The New York Times*, Jan. 17, 1973.

Greenhouse, Linda, "Yonkers Democratic Mayor Finds Reforming City Is a Lonely Job," *The New York Times*, Jan. 7, 1971.

CHAPTER EIGHT: (County) Executive Suite

"Michaelian Job is Enticing Many," *The New York Times*, Jan. 7, 1973.

"Westchester Democrats Top Slate with DelBello," *The New York Times*, March 16, 1973.

"Races Under Way in Westchester – Liberals and Conservatives Offer Major Problems," *The New York Times*, March 25, 1973.

Candreva, Julie, "Ann Janak, Mayor DelBello Tour Town's Sub-standard Housing," *The Patent Trader*, Aug. 11, 1973.

"DelBello Pledges to Seek More State, Federal Help," *The Patent Trader*, Aug. 16, 1973.

"County's Top Race Goes Unnoticed," *The New York Times*, Sept. 30, 1973.

The Daily News (Tarrytown), "Rent Freeze Urged," July 19, 1973.

"DelBello Announces Candidacy for County Executive Position," *The Herald Statesman*, Feb. 28, 1973.

"Rent Freeze Urged," *The Herald Statesman*, July 19, 1973.

"Three Westchester Candidates in Executive Race Open Debate," *The New York Times*, Sept. 8, 1973.

"The Region: Standstill vs. Progress," *The New York Times*, Oct. 14, 1973.

"Three Westchester Candidates in Executive Race Open Debate," *The New York Times*, Sept. 8, 1973.

"New Rent Controls Sought for County," *The Herald Statesman*, March 6, 1973.

"G.O.P. Legislator Backs DelBello for Executive," *The New York Times*, Oct. 11, 1973.

"Meyer Supports DelBello – But Why?", *The Herald Statesman*, Oct. 12, 1973.

Editorial, "DelBello in Westchester," *The New York Times*, Oct. 20, 1973.

Editorial, "For County Executive," *The Herald Statesman*, Oct. 30, 1973.

Feron, James, "Westchester's Democrats Gain Top Post First Time," *The New York Times*, Nov. 8, 1973.

"Cowan Campaign Spends Only $639," *The Reporter Dispatch*, Nov. 3, 1973.

CHAPTER NINE: The Rainmaker

Williams, Lena, "A Look Back at DelBello's 20 Years in Politics," Jan. 13, 1985.

"Michaelian Tangles with Scher, Mayor on Taxes, Welfare," *The Herald Statesman*, Dec. 17, 1971.

Coats, Barbara, "DelBello Lists Top Priorities," *The Patent Trader*, Nov. 24, 1973.

Interview with Michael Spano, Mayor of Yonkers, May 21, 2021.

"New County Executive Seeks Public Help in Confidence Quest," *The Herald Statesman*, Jan. 3, 1974.

"Homebuilding is off Record 37% in Year," *Sunday News*, Feb. 10, 1974.

Feron, James, "DelBello to Reorganize Westchester Bus Links," *The New York Times*, Nov. 9, 1973.

"DelBello Team Won't All Be New," *Gannett Westchester Rockland Newspapers*, Dec. 15, 1973.

"Two-Thirds of a Vote a Westchester Issue," *The New York Times*, March 20, 1974.

"County Board Dems Win 'Veto' Ruling," *The Herald Statesman*, Sept. 11, 1974.

Hoffman, Milton, "DelBello Defends Finance Chief Choice," *The Herald Statesman*, June 24, 1974.

Interview with David Shulman.

"County State Aid Right on the Money," *The Reporter Dispatch*, July 11, 1975.

Dawson, David, "Hospital Funding Vote Due," *Daily News*, March 1, 1976.

"Taking Over 10 Nassau Bus Lines," *The New York Times*, Dec. 28, 1972.

Tritten, Jennie, "Settlement Prospects Brighten as 40,000 Do Without Buses," *The Herald Statesman*, Nov. 10, 1970.

"Five Bus Runs Reinstated," *The Herald Statesman*, Jan. 5, 1974.

"DelBello Eyes Transit Control," *The Herald Statesman*, Jan. 12, 1974.

"Exec Asks Bus Help," *The Herald Statesman*, Feb. 1, 1974.

"DelBello Eyes Transit Control," *The Herald Statesman*, Jan. 12, 1974.

"County Bus Control Passes Hurdle," *The Herald Statesman*, April 4, 1974.

"DelBello Hits Martinelli on Bus Bill," *The Herald Statesman*, May 15, 1974.

"The Bus Problem," *The Herald Statesman*, May 25, 1974.

"County Bus Bill Killed in Albany," *The Herald Statesman*, June 13, 1975.

"M.T.A. Will Begin 'Bus-Rail' Ticket," *The New York Times*, June 18, 1975.

Schweizer, Paul, "DelBello Meets Ford, OK's Transit Bill Cut," *The Daily Item*, Aug. 16, 1974.

Randazzo, John, "Transit Proposals Seen Missing the Bus by 500G," *Sunday News*, April 6, 1975.

Feron, James, "County Control is Urged for Westchester Airport," *The New York Times*, Jan. 26, 1976.

Randazzo, John, "County Seeking More from Airport," July 14, 1974.

Smothers, Ronald, "Pan Am to Run Westchester Field for County For $175,000 a Year," *The New York Times*, Feb. 17, 1977.

"New Airport Landing Guide OK Expected," *The Herald Statesman*, Jan. 14, 1975.

Brian Moss, "'View' Doesn't Shift Safety Views," *The Herald Statesman*, Feb. 20, 1975.

Randazzo, John, "Airport Dispute Lands in Official Laps," *Sunday News*, June 1, 1975.

"Legislature to Set Up a Consumer Agency," *Sunday News*, Sept. 1, 1974.

Editorial, *Westchester County Business Journal*, Jan. 1, 1974.

"DelBello Faces First Political Showdown," *Daily News*, Jan. 9, 1974.

"DelBello Consumer Plan Backed at Public Hearing," *The Herald Statesman*, Feb. 12, 1974.

"Super Battle Looms," *Sunday News*, Feb. 3, 1974.

"DelBello Gets Consumer Boost," *The Herald Statesman*, Feb. 14, 1974.

"Consumer Unit Delayed," *The Herald Statesman*, May 6, 1974.

Feron, James, "DelBello Offers a Consumer Plan," *The New York Times*, June 13, 1974.

"Consumer Unit: Will It Help?" *The Herald Statesman*, March 12, 1975.

"County Board Democrats Hit Consumer Bill Shift," *The Herald Statesman*, July 1, 1975.

"DelBello Hits Changes in Consumer Proposal," *The Herald Statesman*, July 2, 1975.

"Sealer Has Consumer Code Teeth," *The Herald Statesman*, Sept. 10, 1975.

CHAPTER 10: 'Mr. Why Not?' (or Allies and Antagonists)

"Mayor, County Executive Clash," *The Herald Statesman*, Sept. 4, 1974.

Interview with Al DelBello.

"City, County to Work Together," *The Herald Statesman*, Dec. 6, 1974.

Williams, Lena, "Martinelli, Longo Testify in Bias Suit," *The New York Times*, June 17, 1984.

Hoffman, Milton, "Exec, Mayor Take Cases to State Leaders," *The Herald Statesman*, Jan. 30, 1975.

Feron, James, "Supreme Court to Hear Westchester Rent Dispute," *The New York Times*, Dec. 27, 1974.

"DelBello Urges Rent Freeze," *The Herald Statesman*, Jan. 29, 1975.

"Michaelian Tangles with Scher, Mayor on Taxes, Welfare," *The Herald Statesman*, Dec. 17, 1971.

Schweizer, Paul, "Nostalgia, Farewells Fill Council Air," *The Herald Statesman*, Dec. 28, 1973.

Dawson, David, "County Sales Tax Plan Alternative Proposed," *The Herald Statesman*, Dec. 12, 1975.

"The County Executive: He Has a Women's Task Force, But Garbage Gets More Attention," *The Feminist Bulletin*, January 1975.

"No Skirting the Issue at Equal Rights Rally," *Daily News*, Aug. 27, 1975.

Feron, Jeanne Clare, "New Role for Women's Task Force," *The New York Times*, April 9, 1978.

https://women.westchestergov.com/history

Interview with Walter Lipman.

"Westchester Unions Accept 'W.P.A.' Jobs," *The New York Times*, April 20, 1975.

"Job Cuts by GM Pose Crisis in Westchester," *Daily News*, Oct. 27, 1974.

"Job Slide in County to Grow – Nationally, It's Worse," *Sunday News*, Feb. 16, 1975.

Interview with Rev. Jeanette Phillips.

Interview with John Nolon.

Sun River Health website.

"Senior Discounts," *The Herald Statesman*, April 22, 1974.

"Stress Display Senior Citizen Discounts Emblem," *The Herald Statesman*, Oct. 15, 1974.

"DelBello Adds Discount Data," *The Herald Statesman*, Dec. 11, 1974.

"Explanation of Senior Fares," *The Herald Statesman*, Sept. 20, 1975.

"3-Digit Countywide Emergency Number Studied," *The Herald Statesman*, Feb. 18, 1975.

Feron, James, "County Prepares for 911 System," *The New York Times*, May 31, 1987.

Feron, James, "Suburban 911: Where, Exactly, Are You Calling From?" *The New York Times*, Feb. 13, 1991.

Evans, Charlotte, "For the Disabled, A Helping Hand," *The New York Times*, Feb. 15, 1981.

"Westchester Exec Voted Man Most Likely To...," *The Daily Item*, July 11, 1974.

"Top County Executive," *The Herald Statesman*, July 26, 1974.

"DelBello Named Carter Aide," *The Herald Statesman*, Sept. 30, 1976.

http://www.nycroads.com/roads/hutchinson/

Interview with David Shulman.

"Playland Becomes Landmark," *The New York Times*, June 6, 1987.

Whitehouse, Franklin, "Marriott Agrees to Bow Out as Playland's Manager," *The New York Times*, Nov. 2, 1982.

DelBello, Alfred B., "Introduction to the Westchester Community," *The Standard Star*, "Westchester: Communities in Transition Lecture Series," Sept. 26, 1974.

CHAPTER 11: Trash to Cash

Editorial, "Peekskill Plant a Model for Cooperation," *The Journal News*, Oct. 16, 2009.

Martin, Neil S., "DelBello Unveils Waste Proposals," May 8, 1974.

Feron, James, "Westchester Planning to Leave Con Ed," *The New York Times*, July 21, 1976.

Feron, James, "Energy: Is the Breaking Point Near?" *The New York Times*, May 8, 1977.

"Westchester Acts in Garbage Crisis," *The New York Times*, May 9, 1974.

Hoffman, Milton, "County State Aid Right on the Money," *The Reporter Dispatch*, July 11, 1975.

Moran, Nancy, "Garbage Piles Up and Suburbs Seek Place to Put It," *The New York Times*, Aug. 22, 1969.

Solet, Peter, "Garbage Runs $3,000 Daily," June 5, 1969.

Crown, Judith, "Council Threatens Refuse Pullout," *The Herald Statesman*, May 5, 1978.

Schweizer, Paul, "Differences Aired on Refuse Plan," *The Herald Statesman*, June 28, 1974.

"Garbage Transfer Site Gets Board Approval," *The Herald Statesman*, June 26, 1977.

"County Board Votes 16-0 For a Waste-Disposal Network," *The New York Times*, Aug. 20, 1974.

Kates, Brian, "Yonkers Plans to Clean Up on Waste," *Sunday News*, Oct. 27, 1974.

Feron, James, "DelBello Pushes Garbage Proposal," *The New York Times*, July 11, 1974.

Editorial, "A Solid Waste," *The Herald Statesman*, Dec. 13, 1974.

"Councilman Seeks Aid for Waste Plan Battle," *The Herald Statesman*, Jan. 16, 1975.

Cohen, Judd, "Waste Plan Move Gets Another Look," *The Herald Statesman*, Feb. 12, 1975.

Cohen, Judd, "City Gets Waste Demand," *The Herald Statesman*, Feb. 15, 1975.

Cohen, Judd, "County Pushes Haste on Waste," *The Herald Statesman*, June 14, 1975.

Cohen, Judd, "2 Refuse Plans Voted," *The Herald Statesman*, March 12, 1975.

"Sharpe Asks Vote on Garbage," *The Daily Argus*, May 20, 1975.

Connell, Tara, "City Garbage Unit Cost to Triple," *The Daily Argus*, July 29, 1975.

Connell, Tara, "Mount Vernon Picks Own Refuse Plan," *The Daily Argus*, April 29, 1975.

"August P. Petrillo, Mt. Vernon Mayor," *The New York Times*, Aug. 31, 1976.

Jim Striebich, "How Peekskill Solved Westchester's Waste Problem: A Ten-Year Tale of Trash, Sludge, Power and Politics," *Peekskill Herald*, April 8, 2021.

Hoffman, Milton, "County State Aid Right on the Money," *The Reporter Dispatch*, July 11, 1975.

Interview with Alfred B. DelBello.

Smothers, Ronald, "DelBello Assails Con Ed on Waste Plan," *The New York Times*, Nov. 13, 1978.

Smothers, Ronald, "DelBello Presses Solid Waste Plan," *The New York Times*, Feb. 11, 1979.

Smothers, Ronald, "Peekskill Seeking Solid Waste Plant," *The New York Times*, Nov. 16, 1978.

Feron, James, "Westchester Utility Proposition is Defeated," *The New York Times*, Nov. 7, 1979.

Hudson, Edward, "Two Referendums Face Voters on Tuesday," *The New York Times*, March 28, 1982.

Wald, Matthew, "Refuse Project Holds Fiscal Promise," *The New York Times*, Sept. 25, 1983.

Hudson, Edward, "Peekskill Plant Receives First Loads of Garbage," *The New York Times*, Jan. 29, 1984.

Milton Hoffman, "Peekskill Plant a Model for Cooperation," *The Journal News*, Oct. 18, 2009.

Berenyi, Eileen, "Case Study: Westchester County, New York Waste to Energy Facility," Government Advisory Associates Inc.

Wald, Matthew, "Refuse Project Holds Fiscal Promise," *The New York Times*, Sept. 25, 1983.

CHAPTER 12: A New Hospital for Westchester

Feron, James, "Function of New Medical Center Stirs Controversy in Westchester," *The New York Times*, Oct. 26, 1976.

Feron, James, "7-County Hospital Scored at Meeting," *The New York Times*, Sept. 30, 1976.

Feron, James, "Medical Center: It's Ready to Go," *The New York Times*, March 13, 1977.

"WCMC Direction, Operation, Financing Spur Dispute," *Evening Star*, April 2, 1975.

New York Medical College website, nymc.edu.

"Westchester Medical Center 100 Years – A Legacy of Advancing Care," Westchester Medical Center Network, YouTube video.

Feron, James, "Westchester Inquiry Near Completion on Irregularities at Medical Center," *The New York Times*, April 2, 1975.

Feron, James, "Two Westchester Doctors Are Indicted in Lab Fraud," *The New York Times*, May 13, 1975.

"Medical Center Reverts Today to Westchester," *The Standard Star*, May 8, 1975.

Evans, Charlotte, "Westchester Will Shift Control of Clinic," *The New York Times*, Sept. 24, 1979.

Interview with Alfred B. DelBello.

Dawson, David, "Center Crisis Builds," *The Reporter Dispatch*, Nov. 8, 1975.

"County Bonding of Hospital Urged," *Daily News*, Feb. 24, 1976.

Dawson, David, "Hospital Funding Vote Due," *The Reporter Dispatch*, March 1, 1976.

Dawson, David, "Exec Replies to Hospital Questions," *The Herald Statesman*, Oct. 29, 1976.

Feron, James, "Medical Center: It's Ready to Go," *The New York Times*, March 13, 1977.

Feron, James, "Medical Center One Year Later: Still Showing Some Ailments," *The New York Times*, March 12, 1978.

Feron, James, "Conflict Continues Over Medical Center," *The New York Times*, March 12, 1978.

"Dr. George Reed Named a Top Doctor by Marquis Who's Who," Press Release, Marquis Who's Who Ventures LLC, June 14, 2019.

Evans, Charlotte, "New Cancer Unit Opens at County Medical Center," *The New York Times*, Dec. 14, 1980.

Evans, Charlotte, "Westchester Will Shift Control of Clinic," *The New York Times*, Sept. 24, 1979.

Feron, James, "Medical Center Sees the Silver Lining," *The New York Times*, May 27, 1979.

Markham, Pamela, "Supporters Meet to Promote County Burn Center," *The Herald Statesman*, April 1, 1974.

Feron, James, "Westchester Unit on Burns Slated," *The New York Times*, Oct. 20, 1974.

"Burn Center Push Begins," *The Herald Statesman*, Sept. 16, 1974.

DeChillo, Suzanne, "At Burn Center, Painstaking Victories," *The New York Times*, Dec. 18, 1983.

Evans, Charlotte, "New Cancer Unit Opens at County Medical Center," *The New York Times*, Dec. 14, 1980.

Rowe, Claudia, "From County Hospital To Regional Medical Center," *The New York Times*, Feb. 25, 2001.

Brenner, Elsa, "The Medical Center Tests Privatized Waters," *The New York Times*, May 24, 1998.

Foderaro, Lisa W., "Struggling Westchester Hospital Pins Hopes on New Children's Unit," *The New York Times*, June 4, 2004.

CHAPTER 13: Thinning the Blue Line

Feron, James, "Sheriff Plans Suit Over Cut in Budget," *The New York Times*, Nov. 17, 1977.

Ronan, Thomas P., "DelBello and Westchester Sheriff Dispute Over Who Should Head Unified Force," *The New York Times*, Feb. 17, 1978.

Ronan, Thomas P., "Westchester Plans Police Compromise," *The New York Times*, May 5, 1978.

"Westchester is Torn by Police Merger Plan," *The New York Times*, Nov. 6, 1978.

Ronan, Thomas P., "Police Merger Approved 2 to 1," *The New York Times*, Nov. 9, 1978.

Feron, James, "Merger Proposal for Westchester Declared Invalid," *The New York Times*, Feb. 14, 1979.

"Top Westchester Officials Argue Over Inquiry," *The New York Times*, Nov. 9, 1980.

Feron, James, "Delaney Bid to Cite Police Data is Rejected," *The New York Times*, Aug. 2, 1981.

Feron, James, "Judge Cites Political Aspects of Sheriff Case," *The New York Times*, July 5, 1981.

Evans, Charlotte, "Police Head Put on Suspension in Westchester," *The New York Times*, Feb. 24, 1981.

Evans, Charlotte, "Sheriff of Westchester Suspended by DelBello Illegally, Justice Rules," *The New York Times*, March 18, 1981.

Evans, Charlotte, "Court Upholds Suspension of Delaney in Westchester," *The New York Times*, April 4, 1981.

Ungaro, Joseph M., "Our Credibility," *The Reporter Dispatch/ Gannett Westchester Rockland Newspapers*, July 12, 1981.

Evans, Charlotte, "Sheriff Asks for Inquiry on DelBello and His Possible Removal by Carey," *The New York Times*, June 5, 1981.

"Lawman Says Top Cop Had a Booze Problem," *Today*, July 29, 1981.

Feron, James, "Delaney Bid to Cite Police Data is Rejected," *The New York Times*, Aug. 2, 1981.

Feron, James, "DelBello Weighs Jury Report," *The New York Times*, June 21, 1981.

Feron, James, "Sheriff Tied by DelBello to an Accusatory Letter," *The New York Times*, Oct. 2, 1981.

Feron, James, "Board May Urge Negotiated Deal to End Dispute in Delaney Case," *The New York Times*, Dec. 6, 1981.

CHAPTER 14: Enriching Westchester Life

"Westchester Makes Way for the Bicycle," *The New York Times*, June 10, 1974.

Interview with Paul Feiner.

"DelBello Seeking to Prevent Sprawl," *The Record of Yonkers*, March 21, 1974.

"Report Due on County Growth Plan," *The Herald Statesman*, Nov. 20, 1974.

"Environmentalists Quiz DelBello," *Daily News*, Feb. 15, 1974.

"Looking for a Bargain? Try County Parks," *The Herald Statesman*, July 24, 1974.

"Somers' Muscoot Farm Renamed to Honor Late County Executive Al DelBello," *Daily Voice*, Sept. 29, 2016.

"County to Open Crafts, Animal Farm Programs," *The Herald Statesman*, Dec. 12, 1974.

"County Plans Farming Park," *The Herald Statesman*, Sept. 10, 1975.

Feron, James, "Westchester Planning to Abolish Extension Service and Its 4-H," *The New York Times*, Nov. 27, 1974.

Feron, James, "Culture Expands into Suburbs, to Mixed Notices," *The New York Times*, Jan. 9, 1974.

"Briefs on the Arts: DelBello Seeks Cultural Plan," *The New York Times*, Jan. 29, 1971.

"Westchester Opens Art Projects," *The New York Times*, Aug. 25, 1977.

Evans, Charlotte, "Art Program Fills Spaces and Needs," *The New York Times*, Aug 19, 1979.

"Westchester Guide; 'Summerfare' Finale," *The New York Times*, Aug. 8, 1981.

Charles, Eleanor, "Corporate Philanthropy: A Steady, Reliable Income," *The New York Times*, Nov. 2, 1980.

"City Gets Wightman Estate," *The Herald Statesman*, May 9, 1982.

"County Gets Awards for 5 Programs," *The Herald Statesman*, April 15, 1975.

CHAPTER 15: Lockdown

"Valhalla Inmates Seize Cellblocks; No Guards Held," *The New York Times*, July 11, 1981.

Bacerra, Frank Jr., "Lohud Look Back: Inmates Riot at County Jail in 1981," *The Journal News*, Aug. 13, 2019.

Martin, Neil, "Jail Report Spurs Furor," *The Reporter Dispatch*, May 24, 1974.

Feron, James, Westchester Journal, *The New York Times*, April 20, 1980.

https://www.legacy.com/amp/obituaries/dignitymemorial/186639583

Martin, Neil, "County Guards Unhappy," *The Herald Statesman*, Sept. 6, 1974.

Letter from Al DelBello to Stephen Chinlund, chairman, New York State Commission of Correction, Feb. 27, 1981.

An Act to Authorize Institution of Judicial Proceedings Against the State Commission of Correction (draft), 1981.

Memo, Alfred B. DelBello, "Priorities for Jail Overcrowding Task Force," July 9, 1981.

Memorandum of Record from Ted Salem, special assistant to the commissioner, July 2, 1981.

Memo from Sally Birch to Al DelBello and Robert Dolan, July 31, 1981.

http://www.correctionhistory.org/html/chronicl/sheriff/westchester/westchesterjailsorigins08.html

Feron, James, "DelBello Calls Jail Uprising Report 'Distortion'," *The New York Times*, Sept. 27, 1981

Feron, James, "Guards Charged with Brutality in Westchester," *The New York Times*, Feb. 26, 1982.

Haberman, Clyde, "The Lessons of Attica: 25 Years Later," *The New York Times*, Sept. 10, 1996.

Knight, Robert, "Jail Rioters Set 4 Fires in Recent Months," *The Journal News*, Dec. 28, 1973.

Whitehouse, Franklin, "Working to Prevent A Recurrence At Jail," *The New York Times*, July 19, 1981.

Letter, Westchester People's Action Coalition, Inc., Westchester Citizen's Oversight Coalition for Justice in the Jail, July 29, 1981.

Feiden, Doug, "Dramatic Finale to Two-Day Rampage," *New York Post*, July 13, 1981.

Weinstein, Jeremy S., Report of the Senate Minority Crime and Correction Committee, "Westchester Jail Disturbance," Sept. 24, 1981.

Press Release, Tri-County Federation of Police Inc., July 13, 1981.

Letter to The Hon. Alfred B. DelBello from State Sen. Joseph R. Pisani, July 15, 1981.

Letter from Al DelBello to Stephen Chinlund, chairman, New York State Commission of Correction, Feb. 27, 1981.

Letter from Albert D. Gray, Jr., to Stephen Chinlund, chairman, New York State Commission of Correction, Feb. 4, 1981

Greene, Donna, "Pisani: 'I Would Have Gassed Prisoners'," July 18, 1981.

Letter from Alfred B. DelBello to Kevin McNiff, chairman, New York State Commission on Correction, Sept. 4, 1981.

Feron, James, "DelBello Calls Jail Uprising Report 'Distortion'," *The New York Times*, Sept. 27, 1981.

Kriss, Gary, "Crime Index Falls 16.7% in 6 Months," *The New York Times*, Sept. 12, 1982.

CHAPTER 16: Citizen DelBello

Casey, Pat, "DelBello Remembered as a Visionary," *The Examiner News*, May 19, 2015.

Renner, Rom, "Westchester County Association Recalls DelBello," *Daily Voice*, May 8, 2015.

Kitch, Michael, New Hampshire Business Review, "Al DelBello: A 'Pioneer' of Privatization," May 1-15, 1986.

Eddings, Keith, "Lawyer Says DelBello's 2 Roles Don't Present Conflict, *The Journal News*, May 5, 2008.

https://www.yonkerstribune.com/2008/05/al-delbello-con.

Gov. (Andrew) Cuomo Delivers Eulogy at Funeral of Andrew Zambelli, Press Release, Office of the Governor of New York. (https://www.governor.ny.gov/news/audio-video-rush-transcript-governor-cuomo-delivers-eulogy-funeral-andrew-zambelli).

Interview with William M. Mooney Jr.

ABOUT ATMOSPHERE PRESS

Atmosphere Press is an independent, full-service publisher for excellent books in all genres and for all audiences. Learn more about what we do at atmospherepress.com.

We encourage you to check out some of Atmosphere's latest releases, which are available at Amazon.com and via order from your local bookstore:

The Great Unfixables, by Neil Taylor

Soused at the Manor House, by Brian Crawford

Portal or Hole: Meditations on Art, Religion, Race and the Pandemic, by Pamela M. Connell

A Walk Through the Wilderness, by Dan Conger

The House at 104: Memoir of a Childhood, by Anne Hegnauer

A Short History of Newton Hall, Chester, by Chris Fozzard

Serial Love: When Happily Ever After... Isn't, by Kathy Kay

Sit-Ins, Drive-Ins and Uncle Sam, by Bill Slawter

Black Water and Tulips, by Sara Mansfield Taber

Ghosted: Dating & Other Paramoural Experiences, by Jana Eisenstein

Walking with Fay: My Mother's Uncharted Path into Dementia, by Carolyn Testa

FLAWED HOUSES of FOUR SEASONS, by James Morris

Word for New Weddings, by David Glusker and Thom Blackstone

It's Really All about Collaboration and Creativity! A Textbook and Self-Study Guide for the Instrumental Music Ensemble Conductor, by John F. Colson

A Life of Obstructions, by Rob Penfield

Troubled Skies Over Quaker Hill: A Search for the Truth, by Lessie Auletti

ABOUT THE AUTHOR

 **John A. Lipman** is a writer and public policy consultant whose work has appeared in publications such as *The Washington Post, Baltimore Sun,* and *Philadelphia Inquirer.* Lipman served as the chief planner and deputy director of the Cape Cod Commission, an environmental agency of Barnstable County. He also served for three years under Massachusetts governors Weld and Cellucci as the director of growth planning for the Massachusetts Executive Office of Environmental Affairs. He has a B.A. from Bates College, an M.B.A. from Boston University, and a Master of Public Policy from the University of Maryland.

John would like to thank his mother, Doris Lipman, who worked tirelessly for County Executive DelBello and taught him the meaning of tenacity and perseverance.

CPSIA information can be obtained
at www.ICGtesting.com
Printed in the USA
BVHW052133231022
649937BV00003B/12